GOD'S TIMETABLE

STUDIES IN PROPHECY

DAVID BOYD LONG

EVERYDAY PUBLICATIONS

230 Glebemount Avenue
Toronto, Canada   M4C 3T4

ISBN 0-919586-25-2

Cover design by Ken Price

Printed in Canada

INTRODUCTION

Man's timetables are always contingent. Weather, strikes, mechanical failure, bomb threats, hijacking, many things cause frustrations, delay or cancellation. Still it is good to have a plan, but one must remember all man's plans are fragile.

God the Almighty has a timetable for His dealings with men and nothing can upset it. There are many spirit beings who do everything they can to foil God's plan, but they cannot. God's timetable cannot fail.

This new book on prophecy is based on three premises:

1. God is omniscient, He knows the end from the beginning.
2. God is omnipotent, He is well able to carry out His own plans.
3. God has told us something of His plan for man in the Holy Scripture.

David Boyd Long has been studying and teaching God's Word for many years. In this book, with pungent, irreversible argument, Scripture after Scripture is elucidated to substantiate the doctrine that Christ will come for His Church before the great tribulation sets in, before the Millennium. Similarly every stage of God's Timetable is presented with Scriptural authority in a heart warming manner.

God's Timetable

                                                                page

1   God has a Timetable for the World   5
2   God's Timetable for Israel's Future   11
3   God's Timetable in terms of Gentile
     World Empire   20
4   Links between Prophecy in Old and
     New Testaments   29
5   Coming World Rulers - Civil and Religious   34
6   The Coming of the Lord to take the
     Church away   45
7   Final Convulsions of a Dying World   50
9   Future Judgements from God: When?
     Where? Why? Who?   66
10   Christian Rewards   71
11   Christ's Coming in Glory and His
     Kingdom on Earth   79
12   The Eternal State: The sevenfold
     consummation of the purpose of God   87

1   God has a Timetable for the world.

Bible Prophecy is simply God's revealed plan for the future of His creation. This creation, which was once perfect, Gen.1.4 etc., was later marred by the entrance of sin, Gen. 3.17, but has been promised ultimate blessing and perfection through Christ and His work, Roms.8.18-25.

In spite of this declared purpose of God many people seem to feel that events simply drift along, occasionally pushed forward or backward perhaps by men in positions of power. The Christian believes that God is working out His own program at His own pace and according to His own timetable, for he knows that the Bible says, for example:-

The Most High ruleth in the kingdom of men and giveth it to whomsoever He will, Daniel 4.25.

I will overturn, overturn, overturn it ... until he come whose right it is, and I will give it to him, Ezek.21.27.

I will gather all nations against Jerusalem to battle .. then shall the Lord go forth and fight against those nations ... and His feet shall stand in that day upon the mount of Olives ... and the Lord shall be king, Zech. 14.1-9.

The Lord said unto my Lord, Sit thou at my right hand until I make thine enemies thy footstool, Ps.110.1 with Matt.22.44.

God hath put in their hearts (i.e. the confederate kings of Europe) *to fulfil His will ... until the words of God shall be fulfilled, Rev. 17.17.*

These, and many other Scriptures, make clear to the believer that God not only has a plan and a timetable, but that He has given us this timetable in His Word - the Bible. The Old Testament part of this timetable is found most clearly in Daniel 9.24-27, which, in turn, is linked to the New Testament development of the theme in Matthew 24.1-31 by the Lord Himself. This, as we shall see later on in these studies, is amplified, detailed, and carried to consummation in the book of Revelation.

Such a statement, that God has revealed a timetable to us in His Word, frequently evokes a sceptical response, but we believe there is an obvious and fair test for such an affirmation. Such a test might be simply stated in this way: Has God, in the past, committed Himself to any revealed timetable? If so, is it subject to checking and confirmation? Was it adhered to beyond any possibility of coincidence?

If such timetables can be found in the Bible, and if they have been fulfilled as stated above, then we may confidently believe that what God has done in the past He can and will do in the future. We ask the reader to consider a few examples.

Time - Check - Abraham to the Exodus

In Genesis 15.13-16 God gave Abraham the outline of a plan for his descendants which contained a very specific time-check open to confirmation as it unrolled in the future. Read the passage carefully in a good, that is, an accurate translation, and mark its main points.

1) The immediate descendants of Abraham would be strangers (pilgrims) without possessing the land for 400 years from the time of the statement.

2) The whole nation would become slaves. (serve)

3) They would be afflicted and oppressed.

4) The nation so treating them would be punished (judged) by God.

5) This direct invervention of God in judgement would open the way for their liberation (they shall come out).

6) At their liberation they would have "great substance" or wealth, though they had toiled for centuries without pay.

7) In the fourth generation they would "come hither again", that is, they would return to Palestine where the conversation was taking place.

Here, unlike the mumbled doubletalk of the pagan oracles, all is clear, concise, emphatic, and it does not take much Bible research to prove that every one of the seven statements was fulfilled to the letter:-

1) From Genesis 15 to Exodus 12 is 400 years. In Exodus 12.40 we are told that the total period of sojourning was 430, but that would be counted from Abraham's entrance into the land in Genesis 12, thirty years earlier.

2) Though no one could have foreseen slavery for the whole race, yet it actually came about and is historically attested.

3) Even as slaves they were treated with unusual cruelty and oppression in Egypt.

4) God did finally intervene, breaking Egypt's power.

5) Only through that judgement was Israel liberated; not by legislation, change of Egyptian attitude, or revolt of the Israelitish slaves.

6) In spite of more than 200 years of unpaid slavery, Israel did come out with great wealth, because the Egyptians forced this wealth on them to hasten their departure on the night of the Exodus to avert further catastrophe, Ex. 12.35, 36. So great was this wealth that in the desert they later built with it the Tabernacle, lavishly ornamented with gold, silver, and gems which they could never have possessed by any other means.

7) It was in the 4th generation that they were liberated, as God had said; Levi, who went into Egypt with Jacob, followed by Kohath, Amram, and Moses.

This first section of timetable takes us all the way from the covenant with Abraham to the Exodus from Egypt, all meticulously spelled out and all miraculously fulfilled.

Time-Check - Egypt to Canaan

Immediately following the liberation from Egypt we have another prediction by God involving verifiable time factors. The distance from Egypt to Mt. Sinai, approximately 150 miles, was covered in two months by the slow moving horde of probably more than one million people, Ex. 19.1.

They stayed in camp at Sinai about one year, Num. 10.11. There God made His covenant with them, gave them His laws as well as instructions for the building of the Tabernacle, and there this building was made and erected. They left Sinai in the second month of the second year from Egypt, Num. 10.11, and would likely take about the same time, two months, to reach the borders of Palestine at Kadesh-barnea, Num. 12.16; 13.26; 32.8. Here they disobeyed God in refusing to cross over and take possession of the land, staging a rebellion and in their desperation threatening to kill Moses and those who stood with him so that they could "return to Egypt," Num. 14.

Because of this rebellion God said that the whole nation would wander around in the desert for forty years until all over the age of 20 had died; a sentence from which only three men were exempted, Moses, Caleb and Joshua, Num. 14.30. The reason for the number of years - forty - is explained as one year for each day they spent in spying out the land instead of taking God's word for it in faith, Num. 14.33,34.

This prediction was again accurately fulfilled, for not until forty years later did the surviving younger generation cross Jordan into Canaan - led by Joshua and Caleb as God had foretold.

Time-Check - The Babylonian Exile

Many predictions, useful in confirming the accuracy of God's Word, we pass over, because they are not directly connected with the subject of timetables. One very striking time-check, however, appears in connection with Israel's exile in Babylon, and this we urge you to study carefully.

In Leviticus 26:40-45, about 1,500 years before Christ, God told the Israelites through Moses that if they disobeyed His Word He would punish them in a variety of ways. One thing was mentioned specifically, namely, that if they did not allow the land to enjoy its sabbatical rest by lying fallow for one year in seven He would take them away from the land into captivity, so that in their absence the soil would run wild and uncultivated making up in this way for the sabbatical years they had denied it - a year for a year.

After entering Palestine the Hebrew people were ruled by a succession of judges, priests, and prophets for somewhat less than 500 years, and during that time they apparently did not fail in this particular matter. But during the latter period of about 490 years under her kings we gather from several passages that this sabbatical year of land-rest was violated, as indeed were many of God's laws for their well-being.

God remonstrated with His people through the voices of the prophets, without much result, and at last Jeremiah, about the year 496 B.C., brought them a message of judgement from God in Jeremiah 25.8-12. This was to the effect that, since they had refused to listen, and continued to violate the year of sabbath, God was going to do as He had threatened in Leviticus 26 by removing them to Babylon for a period of seventy years.

Again, as at Kadesh-barnea, there is a mathematical justice or retribution in this. In violating for 490 years the one-year-in-seven rule they owed the land 70 years of rest, so God is saying that they will remain in Babylon as exiles for exactly that period. Far from such an exile appearing at that time to be inevitable, a great many false prophets and advisers were busy saying how foolish such a prediction was, and persecuting Jeremiah for continuing to make it. Nebuchad-nezzar had invaded Palestine twice in the preceding years and still everything was going on much as usual in the land, so the false prophets prophesied "Peace, peace!" and there was little sign that God would keep His word and send Israel into exile.

Yet six years or so later the Babylonish armies came on a final military operation. They captured and dethroned the king, deported the mass of the population to Babylon and scorched the land with fire and sword, leaving it a desolation where little but wild animals remained and these in time took over whole areas of it. The keeper of the national chronicle writing by divine inspiration in 2 Chronicles 36.20,21 says that all this was done so that the land might make up her lost sabbatical years *in fulfilment of the word of the Lord by the mouth of Jeremiah.*

God's Word was again fulfilled to the letter, as it had been in the previous instances, and they remained in Babylon for 70 years until God overthrew that nation by bringing the Medes against them. Later, with a change of dynasty a Persian king called Cyrus allowed the Jews to return to their land exactly 70 years after their deportation. Jeremiah, who had remained in the land with a small and poor remnant, understood this timetable. So did the writer of 2 Chronicles 36.22, and so did Daniel who was one of the deportees, Dan.9.2.

Another Timetable

And at this precise moment when this timetable was running to a close, God gave Daniel another timetable involving another period of 490 years of Israeli national history which would carry right through to the coming of Messiah and His rejection and "cutting off" by His own people; the subsequent destruction of the holy city by the Romans, and then, after a long period of dispersion, to the kingdom of Messiah and the consummation of God's plans for Israel and the whole earth.

Surely, if as we have seen God has so meticulously kept to all His other revealed timetables we have no reason to doubt that He will keep to this last one given to us in Daniel 9 and which we shall consider in the next chapter.

God's Timetable for Israel's Future

2

Our last study showed clearly that in connection with the early history of Israel God had worked to a timetable and that this timetable had been revealed and spelled out ahead of time, in some cases hundreds of years ahead.

We cited three examples of this, namely:

a) From the covenant with Abraham in Genesis 15 to the liberation from Egypt, covering 400 years, with seven specific sections in the prediction, all fulfilled exactly as promised.

b) From the revolt at Kadesh-barnea, Num. 13, to the entrance into Canaan under Joshua and Caleb - 40 years, exactly as promised.

c) From the desolation of Jerusalem by the armies of Babylon to the return of the exiles under Ezra in the days of Cyrus of Persia - 70 years exactly as promised, Ezra 1.1; 2 Chron. 36.20,21; Jer. 25.8-12.

With this in mind we are not surprised when God does the same again in Daniel 9, with a timetable which links the last of these three earlier periods with the latter days of Israel's history. This one in Daniel 9 covers the whole national course of Israel from the return to the land under Ezra and Nehemiah, through the first coming and death of Messiah, to the Great Tribulation and final repentance of the nation leading to her blessing in the Kingdom under that same Messiah returned to earth in glory.

A *pivotal passage*

Some of the program has already been fulfilled (from the rebuilding of Jerusalem under Nehemiah, to Messiah) and is therefore open to checking and confirmation. The major portion of the prophecy has already been fulfilled completely and precisely and we can assume that the remainder will be fulfilled. Because of this, Daniel 9 must be one of the most important pivot passages in the whole prophetic Scriptures, and should be examined with great care.

Beginning at Daniel 9.2 we read about Darius, the son of Ahasuerus, who had overthrown Nebuchadnezzar's grandson to start the Medo-Persian supremacy and thus prepare the way for the restoration plan which God had for Israel.

> *In the first year of his reign, I Daniel understood by books* (the Scriptures) *the number of years whereof the word of the Lord came to Jeremiah the prophet, that He would accomplish seventy years in the desolations of Jerusalem,* Daniel 9.2.

In these words Daniel links the 70-year program of desolations just about to close, with his prayer in this chapter, and with God's revelation to him of the timetable for the succeeding period of Israel's history. He prayed in this way because in Deuteronomy 30 where God had foretold these very judgements He had also spoken in anticipation of Israel's repentance. There in verses 1-3 God says that if they turned to Him in repentance He would hear them and restore them to their land. With this is mind Daniel's prayer is one of repentance and confession on behalf of the nation, and an appeal for restoration.

In the same passage of Deuteronomy (30.3-10) Moses goes on to foretell the *ultimate* blessing of Israel in terms which we know from other passages will only be fulfilled in Messiah's kingdom. It seems probable that Daniel jumped to the conclusion that once Israel returned to their land from Babylon at the end of the 70 years of desolations, these Messianic and universal blessings of the kingdom would begin. This is not specifically stated, but it seems to be assumed in the words of the angel sent to give him *instruction, insight, and understanding,* thus correcting his mistake.

In verse 24 this angel sees that 70 *weeks* (of years), and not merely 70 years, would be necessary, and had actually been determined or appointed by God on Daniel's people, to round out their national history by bringing in Messiah's Kingdom.

Seven steps to ultimate blessing

In this verse seven momentous matters are to be brought to consummation in this given period of time which we shall study in detail later on. It is enough to remark just now that all seven are connected with *thy people* (Israel) and *thy holy city* (Jerusalem), so that neither the church nor the church age is in view in these Scriptures.

In the passage seven sevens (of years) are determined on Israel -

1) To finish transgression.
2) To make an end of sin.
3) To make reconciliation (atonement) for iniquity.
4) To bring in everlasting righteousness.
5) To seal up the vision.
6) To seal up the prophecy.
7) To anoint the Most Holy.

Like almost all other lists of seven in the Scriptures the middle one (No. 4) here is the pivot and key. Undoubtedly Christ's work on the cross laid the foundation for everlasting righteousness in every sphere, at every level, and in every context, but the laying of a foundation is one thing while the actual *bringing in* of the condition in a manifest way, is quite another.

To illustrate this, Christ procured salvation in its broadest sense at the cross, making it available to all men, yet not all men accept it, and many verses of the Bible show that in its ultimate fulness *salvation* is something looked forward to in the future even by those who are now saved by faith, Rom. 13.11; 1 Pet. 1:5,9 etc. The bringing in of *everlasting righteousness* in our verse clearly refers to its being established on earth in a visible and practical way, and that in connection with Israel and her kingdom, Isa.60.21; Psalm 72.7; Isa.1.26; 33.5 etc.

All still future

We suggest that a glance down the other items on the list will quickly convince the open minded that not only has the middle one never been fulfilled, but that not one of the seven has ever been fulfilled as stated, in relation to Israel. In these seven points we have a summary of God's program for the ultimate blessing of Israel and, through her, of the whole earth.

In the remainder of the passage we have God's timetable for the completion of that plan which will not be completed until Israel's transgression, sin, and iniquity have been dealt with and put away, until universal righteousness has been permanently established throughout the whole kingdom of God, until God's seal has been put on the total fulfillment of all the picture language of Old Testament visions, and on all the oral and written communications of the prophets, and until the Most Holy has been anointed. This last could mean either the public anointing of Messiah as king or, more probably, the anointing of the sanctuary of the millennial Temple as the centre of all the worship of earth.

A week is seven years

The term *seventy weeks* in verse 24 of Daniel 9 is literally *seventy sevens*. Technically these could be *sevens* of anything, the context being always the deciding factor. *A seven* was the Hebrew unit for counting or expressing groups of things, as we in English use the terms *a couple, a dozen, a score,* etc. A Sabbath marked off a group of seven units of time. This could be of days, as in the weekly Sabbath; of weeks or months as in the feasts; of years, as in the sabbatical year of rest for the land; or in groups of seven years, as in the year of Jubilee (the year following seven sevens of years, i.e., the 50th year. See Lev.25.1-10.)

The context in Daniel 9 is clearly one of years, since he

was praying about restoration to the land after a period of seventy years in captivity. The angel says, in effect, "Not seventy years are necessary, but seventy sevens or weeks of years will be required to bring God's plan for national restoration to conclusion." That is, 490 instead of 70.

This time span of 490 years is a significant one, and well marked in Israel's past history. In round terms:

From the covenant with Abram to the entrance into Canaan was 490 years.

From that point to the beginning of monarchy under Saul was 490 years.

From the monarchy's beginning to the captivity in Babylon was 490 years.

God is now saying that from the restoration after that captivity to their final millennial glory under Messiah would be a fourth such 490 year period. It is at least interesting that this total time span of Israel's history is thus close to 2,000 years, as the church's has almost run that long, and, according to internal Biblical chronology, Abram entered Canaan almost 2,000 years from Adam.

The starting point

In this timetable outlined to Daniel the starting point for the 490 years is clearly and precisely stated, as is the terminus. The beginning of the whole period is given as *the going forth of the commandment to restore and build Jerusalem*, v.25. There is only one such command in Scripture, and that was given by Artaxerxes to Nehemiah in Nehemiah 2.1-9, and it was specifically authorization *to build and restore Jerusalem*. The date is given as Nisan of the 20th year of the king's reign, and this is a date easily confirmed from secular history as Nisan (March) of the year B.C. 445.

According to verse 25, from that date *to Messiah the prince* would be 483 years, or 69 weeks of 7 years each. This was again divided into two periods, one of seven sevens, or 49 years which was taken up with the job of building and restoring the city, and the second was of 434 years, or 62 sevens down to the appearing of the Anointed One who would, of course, bring in the glorious kingdom. God had, therefore, committed Himself to a clear and detailed schedule up to the Messiah. Did He, in fact, keep to it? The answer is an unqualified *Yes*.

As we have said, the first span of 49 years covered the whole period of the rebuilding of the Jewish capital, with the many interruptions mentioned in the book of Nehemiah. It was indeed finished with streets, walls and a moat, v.25 (NASV) *in times of distress*. At the end of the 69 sevens Messiah was to be *cut off and have nothing* (NASV). Sir Robert Anderson has worked out, with the help of the Astronomer Royal at Greenwich Observatory, through lunar calculations that from the 1st Nisan 445 B.C. to Messiah's entry into Jerusalem, 6th April A.D.32, on the donkey as foretold by the prophets was exactly 483 years of twelve 30 day (lunar) months. For the details of these calculations see "The Coming Prince" by Sir R. Anderson, page 128. He was then *cut off,* Isa.53.8, and although He had *come to His own [kingdom]* He was rejected, and died *with nothing* in relation to His visible or material kingdom.

One wonders how the Jewish people, and in particular their so meticulous Bible interpreters could read all this and much more in the Old Testament, and still not believe that Jesus was the Christ, their Messiah.

So we see that so far God has kept to His timetable with the utmost precision through the 483 years from the decree of Artaxerxes to the crucifixion of the Lord, just as He had throughout the previous timetables to which He had committed Himself. And this leaves us with one week, or seven years, of Israel's *national* history to be investigated to bring us to the culmination of God's plan for them in the universal reign of Christ.

Prophecies of Israel

At this point we would draw attention to a statement earlier in this chapter to the effect that all this relates to the Jewish people, their land, their city, their Messiah, and their kingdom. The church nowhere figures in it, for the church is not the subject of Old Testament Prophecy, nor indeed of

Old Testament revelation. In the New Testament the church is called a *mystery,* that is, something not previously revealed but now communicated to us. It follows that the whole church period, being one of grace when Israel is "put away" or "broken off," Rom.11, is not included in these calculations. We are in *the times of the Gentiles,* Luke 21.24, when Israel's national clock is, so to speak, stopped. It will only be re-started when the church is removed and God begins to deal with Israel again *as a nation.*

If further proof were needed for this statement, it may be found in the fact that in Daniel 2 and Daniel 7 the judgement of God, which sweeps away the Gentile sovereignty to make room for Messiah's kingdom, comes at a time when the final world empire, a revival of the Roman, is in the form of a ten-kingdomed federation. This is seen in the ten toes of the image and the ten horns of the fourth beast, and is found so interpreted of the ten-horned beast in Revelation 17.12. Whatever forms the Roman Empire may have had in the past, or indeed the area covered by it at any time, it has never been in that of a federation of ten kings or rulers, though we see foreshadowings in our day of how this could come about. So the final week of seven years which will lead directly up to the enthroning of the Lord Jesus on earth, has to be looked for at the end of the church age.

The coming prince

To return to our timetable, we find that following the cutting off of Messiah *the people of the prince that shall come will destroy the city and the sanctuary. And its end will come with a flood; even to the end of the war desolations are determined,* Dan.9.26. And so it transpired historically. Less than 40 years after the crucifixion, the Roman armies under Titus, at the end of a long and bitter siege poured into the city like a devastating flood, tearing down the city and the Temple stone from stone, crucifying the Jews in thousands and carrying off the sacred vessels and furnishings of the Holy Place as booty of war. Thus began the greatest and most terrible of Jewish scatterings - or Diaspora - which has continued across 19 centuries of suspended national existence, right to our own day.

The prince that shall come refers to the future head of the revived Roman Empire of whom we shall see more in future studies. He, personally, is not in view yet in our passage, but it was *his people,* the Romans, who desolated Jerusalem in A.D.70, exactly as God had foretold to Daniel.

This sacking of Jerusalem terminates the 69th week of years (483 years from the beginning of the rebuilding) and leaves one week still future, that is seven years. It is the dramatic seven year period stretching over the whole span from the signing of a treaty with the head of the Roman Empire after the removal of the church, until the setting up of the kingdom of Messiah. See Daniel 9.27.

We shall leave details of that future period for our next study and merely refer to what is said of it here. This is condensed into one verse which tells us that the coming world ruler (the prince) will confirm a pact with Israel, by that time regathered in the land though still in unbelief and unrepentant as we see her today. This pact, probably a defensive one, will be to aid the Jewish nation against her neighbours who will be then as they are now her antagonists. Chief of these will be the King of the North (the great Communist federation of the last days), the King of the South (Egypt, and possibly another group of nations of which she will be head), and the Kings of the East (Israel's enemies just east of the Euphrates). Read Daniel 11.36-45 with Ezekiel 38, with Revelation 12,13 and 17.12-17.

This pact, entered into for a period of seven years, is violated by the prince's suspension of the sacrifices and the meal offerings. At this point appears the ominous phrase *the abomination which causes desolation* first mentioned in Daniel 9.27, then in 12.11, and later cited by the Lord Jesus Christ in Matthew 24.15. This citation, by the way, links up the prophecies of the Old Testament with those of the New, and this act by the great dictator in the middle of the week is clearly stated by the Lord Jesus as being the starting point of the Great Tribulation, Matthew 24.15-21.

At this critical point Israel is faced with the choice of allowing the desecration of the Temple; worshipping this image; accepting the mark of the Beast in token of complete submission to him, or else of refusing to do any of these and making themselves the objects of his furious persecution in a slaughter unprecedented in world history, Matt. 24.21. This is, in fact the Great Tribulation which we shall study in detail in a later chapter. At this point we have been merely establishing the fact of God's timetable and noting the overall movement of it.

God's Timetable in terms of Gentile World Empire

3

Having followed God's program strictly as it refers to Israel, we must now notice that He has also given us a number of clear, though condensed, outlines of Gentile world rule leading up to its final destruction, which will make way for Christ's universal dominion as Son of Man.

Two of these outlines are given to us in Daniel chapters 2 and 7, and this is fitting and significant because Daniel lived at one of the great intersections of history. It is also worth noticing that, in the original, the whole section from 2.4 to 7.28, is written, not in the Hebrew language of the Israelites, but in Aramaic, the language of the Gentile Babylonians, thus calling attention to its importance to Gentiles as well as Jews.

When God settled His people in His land of Palestine He made Jerusalem not only His seat and home but also His world capital. Other nations, because of their incorrigible wickedness were *given over* (Rom. 1.24,26,28), and no longer dealt with directly by God. But Israel, in turn, departed from God, refusing to be recalled by the prophets and finally, because of her sins, was torn from her land and carried into exile, first the ten tribes to Assyria, and later Judah into Babylon, as we have seen. Thus began *the times of the Gentiles*, Luke 21.24, with God's centre of rule passing from Israel to pagan kings in whose hands it would remain until the coming of Christ, who is to set up His throne in Jerusalem and from there rule throughout the world. So it is entirely fitting that at this precise moment when He had just given world rule to the Gentiles He should outline the course of Gentile world rule from beginning to end, especially as it impinged on Israel's history and led up to the final restoration under Messiah.

The times of the Gentiles

In figurative language God gave two outlines of the whole course of *the times of the Gentiles*. One is in Daniel 2 and was given to a pagan monarch, Nebuchadnezzar, who was then at the head of world power. The other, in chapter 7, is given to a Hebrew prophet, Daniel. The first is man's view of this portion of history, the second is God's. So in the first, Gentile world rule is seen as a beautiful and symmetrical work of art, worthy of admiration, and extremely valuable.

In the second picture, given in Daniel 7 to the prophet, the viewpoint is God's, as is the evaluation. So man's rule on earth is seen, not as a magnificent and monolithic work of art, but rather as four ravening wild animals tearing and being torn, until finally *the judgement of God shall sit and they shall take away his dominion* (that is, of the last king) *to consume and destroy it to the uttermost*, Dan.7.26. But we must look at the two descriptions in more detail. First, King Nebuchadnezzar's dream.

Gentile world rule as seen by man

From the golden head to the feet of mixed iron and clay we see, in the king's great image, four great world empires succeeding each other, as they overcome and absorb each its predecessor. Babylon and its king is said to be the head of gold. Then comes the trunk of silver which, with its two arms, represents the dual nature of the Medo-Persian Empire, first under the Medes, then dominated by the Persians. Next we have the *belly and thighs of brass* which are not here identified by name though we know that, historically, Greece followed Medo-Persia in world rule, led by Alexander of Macedon. And in Daniel 8.20-21, in yet another picture of these competing nations, the ram is said to stand for Medo-

Persia while the conquering he-goat is plainly said to be *the kingdom of Grecia*. The fourth great world power, represented in the legs of iron, is, of course, the Roman Empire.

While impressive at first sight, a closer scrutiny shows deterioration all the way from gold to miry clay; from magnificence to mud; from monolithic centralized power in the golden head to an unstable mixture of iron and clay, elements which never really fuse and cannot cohere. The structure is top heavy, vulnerable, and at its very foundation rests on its most brittle part, and also its weakest.

We see a further process of weakening and lack of cohesion in the fact that while Nebuchadnezzar and the golden head represented unity and absolutism, there was division under the Medes and Persians whose kings were shackled by *the laws of the Medes and Persians* so that even Darius could not save Daniel though he wanted to do so, Dan.6.14,15. This lack of unity was further seen in Alexander's great empire which, though so vast and so speedily won was nonetheless unassimilated, unwieldy, barely kept in submission, constantly in upheaval, and at his death divided into four kingdoms among his generals who became its kings.

The Roman empire too, as indicated in the legs of the image, divided into East and West with its rival capitals in Rome and Constantinople constantly at war with each other. Just before the coming of Christ to destroy the whole system it will be further divided as indicated in the ten toes, which are said to be ten kings, Dan.2.44, in whose days the destruction would take place. Compare also Daniel 7.23,24 and Revelation 17.12-17. In spite of its outward grandeur, all is deteriorating, weak, brittle, lacking in unity and cohesiveness, and also ripe for destruction and ready to crumble at the blow from God.

Non-unity today

We see this very characteristic before us today in preparation for the end. Never was there more talk of unity, and the grandiose names and titles of it are everywhere: United Nations, World Council of Churches, International Federation of Labour, World Bank, World Monetary Organization, NATO, SEATO, E.E.C., Afro-Asian Block, Pan-American Organization etc. And never was there less of the desired unity even within what is called "United Nations" and indeed every other grouping of men. Almost every nation great and small is wrestling with divisions and secessionist movements. F.L.Q. in Canada as well as the more politically minded Separatists, Irish, Welsh and Scottish nationalist parties in the U.K., Flemings and Walloons, Basques, Andorreans etc. in Western Europe, while in Eastern Europe only massive and bloody repressions keep Croats, Slovenes, Austrians, Czechs, Hungarians, Poles etc. in any kind of administrative unity. And on the inside every nation, group, and party is rent and sectionalized by age groups, cultures, colours, ideologies, economics, politics, etc.

We have cultures, counter-cultures, sub-cultures, money-cultures, drug-cultures etc. And the divisions and antagonisms run right through our society, our educational systems, our home and family relationships at the very foundations of world structure. All is summed up in Daniel 2.43, *Whereas thou sawest iron mixed with miry clay, they shall mingle themselves....but they shall not cleave one to another even as iron is not mixed with clay.*

One thing becomes clear as we study this chapter, namely, the last empire of iron is seen in existence at the second coming of Christ, for it is on these very ten toes, or ten kings, that the Coming Stone falls, bringing the whole structure to an end. This means that whatever gaps there may be in the picture, and we shall explain at least one presently, the image represents the whole course of the *times of the Gentiles,* from its beginning *to its end.* From Nebuchadnezzar to the ten-kingdomed form at the conclusion, all falls in complete destruction and disappears, being swept away *like chaff from the summer threshing floor* at the coming of Christ, the stone rejected by Israel's builders but now become their Rock and the Capstone of their history. There is no Gentile power after this, all is gone and the world is in subjection to God's Anointed, Dan. 2.35.

Similarly in Daniel 7, where the last empire is pre-figured by a beast with ten horns, which are said to be ten kings, v.24, all is again swept away, *consumed and destroyed to the uttermost*, 7.26, and the kingdom of Christ which follows it has no successor, for it is *forever*. So we are studying the total winding up of all Gentile rule.

Some may wonder why Gentile world rule is not traced farther back, say, to Egypt, Syria, or Assyria. The answer is that here God is dealing with world powers as they touch on the history of His people during the dispersion, the times of the Gentiles, when rule has been taken from Israel and given to Gentiles. This also accounts for the dropping out of the image anything that would represent the period of the Church, when Israel is set aside, Roms. 9 and 10, with her clock stopped and her history as a nation in abeyance.

The Standing Monument

So the imposing monument of Gentile world rule stands before us today, with the golden head period of Babylonia superseded and absorbed by the silver breast and arms of Medo-Persia, and this, in turn, by the brass of Greece, and the iron of Rome. And when it is fully displayed in all its completed splendor its moment of doom has come, for *a stone cut out without hands*, i.e. unlike the image, not of human origin, comes from heaven, and in one crushing blow of Divine judgement brings the whole structure crashing in rubble. As we have said the stone is Christ and His kingdom, which kingdom then grows until it becomes universal, *filling the whole earth*. We learn from later portions, and from other Scriptures, the different instruments God will use in this overthrow. Here we are merely given the fact and the consequences.

We also note in our passage that nothing of the structure or material of men's kingdoms is carried over or incorporated into God's. The whole fabric is shattered, carried away like chaff before a gale, *and no place was found for it*, Dan.2.35. When the Medes overthrew the Babylonish empire and took over the supreme rule and authority, Babylon was not annihilated, did not disappear. It continued to live on as a component of the new empire, though not a ruling one, and much of its culture, organization, art, and even language etc. was absorbed and adopted, as happened, in turn all down the line. But when God overthrows the rule of man He will adopt or absorb nothing. He will destroy it and nothing will remain or have a *place* in the new thing which He will establish. His kingdom will be heavenly in character.

Gentile world rule as seen by God

We now turn to chapter 7 where God reveals to the Hebrew prophet His own view of Gentile dominion throughout its whole course.

In verses 3 and 4 we see four wild beasts coming up out of the Great or Mediterranean Sea. These beasts represent the same four great Gentile world empires as we have seen in the great image. Yet even here we see the power of God behind the scenes at work for His own purposes, for it is as a result of the working of the "four winds of *heaven*" that the beasts rise up. The railing sea is a picture of the surging masses of Gentile mankind around the shores of the Mediterranean area, but God is stirring it all and bringing up those who will, often unconsciously, work out His will and purpose: a Nebuchadnezzar who will punish His people for their sins by taking them away into exile; a Darius who will bring down the arrogance of the Babylonians for overstepping His orders; a Cyrus of Persia who will release His people and help them to go back to their land exactly at the end of the seventy years marked out and foretold by God. It is worth noting that Cyrus had been mentioned *by name* in Isaiah 44.28 and 45.1-5 more than 100 years before his birth.

Even the advent of the Romans as a world power was brought about by God Himself to prepare the way and the world for the first coming of Christ, and, by its unifying influence and language, for the spread of the Gospel as it could not otherwise have spread. The very location of the birth of Christ, as foretold to take place in Bethlehem, was made possible by an edict of Caesar Augustus, for Joseph and Mary lived in Nazareth and not Bethlehem, Luke 2.1-4.

The four winds and four beasts remind us of their universal or world-wide character. But in the image these kingdoms are seen as a creation of man and viewed from man's standpoint. Here in chapter 7 their moral character is displayed rather than their mere succession or their administrative systems, and it is God's viewpoint throughout. They are wild ravaging animals, tearing and destroying each other in a mad lust for dominance.

Four beasts

First is the winged lion, and this has been the emblem and crest of Babylon even by her own choice. Everywhere in the archaeological excavations around Babylon this same winged lion is prominent as the symbol of the king and his empire. But here as elsewhere there is deterioration, for his wings are plucked; his power curtailed, or at least his speed, and he stands up like a man and acts as with a man's heart. A lion acting like a man and with a man's feelings is a poor beast indeed, tame and restrained with little of his wild and kingly character. In other words he is no longer his independent, dictatorial, regal self. He is soft hearted and inspires the same kind of pity one feels for a once-feared bear who now tamely dances to amuse children for a hand-out of sugar lumps. This is the decadence of Babylon as seen in the difference even between Nebuchadnezzar and his grandson Belshazzar.

Next comes a great bear, neither regal nor swift, but overwhelming and crushing in spite of its ambling gait. And such was the Medo-Persian might. The beast has three ribs in its teeth which Keil and others take to represent Babylon, Lydia, and Egypt which had already fallen prey to the gluttonous rapacity of the Medes. For the Medo-Persian nation was far inferior in culture and character to the Babylonians, but far more covetous and overwhelming. The words of verse 5, *Arise, devour much flesh*, are very fitting, for, according to historians who have studied the matter widely and deeply, there has rarely been seen on earth a horde so cruel and destructive, or on such a scale as this.

The leopard with four heads and four wings is clearly the

Greek empire with incredible speed of conquest under its four generals who later inherited the four quarters of that empire on Alexander's death. The four generals would be represented by the four wings of flying victory, and later on were its four heads as its rulers. Their names were, Cassander who took over Macedon and Greece; Seleucus who took Syria and Upper Asia; Lysimachus who ruled over Asia Minor and Thrace; while Ptolemy seized Egypt, Palestine, and Arabia. Tatford draws attention to the fact that the first three beasts here are those mentioned by Jehovah in Hosea 13.7-8, *I will be to them as a fierce* lion, *as a* leopard *I will lurk for them in the way; I will meet them as a* bear *bereaved of her whelps,* and goes on to say that the words of verse 8 may refer to the fourth wild beast of our passage, "the *wild beast* of the field shall tear them."

The fourth beast

In verse 7 of Daniel 7 the fourth and last of the world empires is pictured as *a fourth beast, dreadful and terrible, strong exceedingly, and it had great iron teeth. It devoured and brake in pieces....it was diverse from all the beasts that went before it; AND IT HAD TEN HORNS.* Here again we have the appearance of the Roman Empire, but marked by God to go on to a phase when it is a ten-kingdom confederacy, something it has never been up to the present. The ten horns seen here on the beast answer to the ten toes of the image, and represent the final stage, just before the stroke of doom falls on it. It will be noted that in each of the successive visions of Daniel we have details not given in the previous one, each detail calling attention to some important feature.

In keeping with that principle God, in this vision, goes on to show us that among the ten future kings of the coming empire comes up another, making eleven. But this eleventh proceeds to overthrow three of the others; takes their place; goes on growing and pushing until he completely dominates the whole scene. Now, at last, things are being focussed clearly and we are pre-viewing the last great world dictator, the one who will take over in the western world and lead its armies directly and personally against the Son of God and His people in the final showdown of Armageddon. See Revelation 19.19.

The horn

Whatever stream of prophecy we follow: Dan.7, Dan. 9.27,28, Dan.11.36-45, Matt.24.15-21, 2 Thess.2.3-10, Rev. 13.1-10; 17.12-18; 19.19, each one leads us ultimately to this sinister personality, Satan's viceroy on earth. He is called in different places The Horn, The Beast, The Man of Sin, The Son of Perdition, The Wicked One etc. He makes himself supreme over traditions and laws, and all is given into his hand for *a time, and two times, and half a time* which is the three and a half *times* or half of the final and fateful week of seven years we have already noticed in Daniel 9 which will bring Israel's history to its consummation. He brings in the Great Tribulation, *making war against the saints. He speaks great words against the Most High.* In Daniel 9.27 this dictator-prince makes a defence pact with Israel for one week of seven years, but violates it by setting up *the abomination which makes desolate in the midst of the week,* i.e., at the three and a half year mark. This is the crisis point at which we must pause, for the Lord Jesus emphatically says that this act is that which sets in motion the horrors of "the Great Tribulation," Matt.24.15-22. So all our Scripture studies so far lead us to one dreadful personality, to one momentous crossroads in world history, and to one moment of crisis. This we shall study in another chapter.

4 Links between Prophecy in Old and New Testaments

We have already referred to different streams of prophecy and there are many, but they all meet in the book of Revelation, and in that book all the plans of God come to fruition. In spite of Hell's most determined opposition God is there seen as victorious, and the whole tapestry is completed, with threads drawn from far back in the ages of the Old Testament prophets.

But can we be sure of the connections? Were they, in fact, outlining this same plan which is completed in the New Testament? Are the personalities the same? The Beast, that coming prince-leader of the great rebellion; the Son of Man; the saints of the Most High who take the kingdom and reign forever; are we sure of being on the right track? To these questions we must now turn our attention.

Ten toes - ten horns - ten kings

In the very first outline of Gentile world rule, given in Daniel 2, we see the whole structure of that Empire ending in the ten toes of the image, part iron and part clay. They are, in that passage, specifically called *these kings* and doom comes in their days. Next in chapter 7 we have the final form of world rule in the fourth beast which has ten horns, and of them God Himself says in verse 24, *the ten horns out of this kingdom are ten kings that shall arise.* Then in Revelation 13 we read of a beast aspiring to dethrone God and take over world sovereignty and again he has ten horns, and the horns are *crowned.* Almost all that is said of this beast in Revelation is taken practically word for word from Daniel.

These same ten horns appear again in Revelation 17.3 where we see a woman called *Babylon* riding a beast with ten horns. In verse 12 God says, *The ten horns....are ten kings which have received no kingdom as yet but receive power* (exousia - delegated authority) *as kings for one hour* with the beast. *These have one mind and give their power* (exousia as above) *and strength to the beast.* In verse 17 we read, *God has put in their hearts to fulfil His will and to agree and to give their kingdom to the Beast until the words of God shall be fulfilled.* Again in Revelation 19.19 without using the number 10 God tells us that at the very point of their destruction in the Lake of Fire the Beast and the kings of the earth and their armies gathered together to make war against Him who sat on the horse, i.e., the Lord Jesus Christ.

In all these Scriptures we have the same ten kings, completely dominated by one of their number who speaks blasphemies against God, attempting to usurp His place. In each case they are represented as the final form of human government on earth, humanism having reached its ultimate peak in the attempted deification of man in the place of God. And in each case they are destroyed by direct Divine intervention. There can be no doubt about their identity.

The super dictator

As we advance we find in Daniel 7 that among the ten is one who overthrows three, takes their place and finally dominates the whole scene and movement. Shortly he is found in direct and personal combat with God and all that God stands for.

In Daniel 9.26 this leader of the last days is called *the prince who is to come.* In that passage we find Israel making a treaty or pact with him for defence against her attackers from the north and south. He is there for the first time connected with *the desolating abomination* and the cutting off of the daily sacrifice.

He appears again in Daniel 11.36 where, among other

things, he speaks *marvellous things against the God of gods,*
as in 7.25, showing that this is the same person. We find this
individual again in 2 Thessalonians 2, Revelation 13.1-10;
17.12,13; and 19.19. In each case the characteristics, the activities, the position, and the doom are described in almost
identical words, forming a series of very strong links in an
unbreakable chain of prophetic truth.

The Olivet discourse

Undoubtedly the strongest link of all is that of Matthew
24 where the Lord Himself gives an outline of prophecy in
answer to a question from the disciples as to what would be
the sign of His coming and of the end of the age.

From verses 4 to 6 He outlines preliminary rumblings of
false Christs and wars but adds, *Be not troubled, the end is
not yet.* In verses 7 and 8 He speaks of *famines, pestilences
and earthquakes* and calls these *the beginning of sorrows,*
referring to the first half of Israel's last momentous week of
years. In verse 14 He speaks of bitter persecution and the
world-wide preaching of the Gospel of the Kingdom. This last
reminds us that at this time Israel is back in centre stage
again and that this is a parallel to Revelation 7 where the
witnesses are no longer those of the church, but are a great
company taken from among *all the tribes of Israel.* After this
Christ says, *Then cometh the end,* meaning not that there will
be nothing more happening, but that what happens leads to
the consummation of Israel's history. When will *the end*
come? *When you see the desolating abomination spoken of
by Daniel the prophet standing in the sanctuary.*

From this it is quite clear that however harrowing may be
the sorrows of Israel and the world during the first part of this
period, *the Tribulation, the great one* only begins with the
setting up of something causing defilement and desolation in
the very Temple of God. Christ says this was spoken of by
Daniel the prophet, and the reference is to Daniel 9.27, and
12.11. In the first place it is connected with the violation, by
the prince, of the treaty with Israel in the middle of the week
of seven years.

Another interesting point of comparison linking prophetic passages is seen in the exact parallel between the Seven Seals of Revelation 6 and the signposts given by the Lord in Matthew 24.5-21. These can be studied better if arranged in columns:

Matthew 24	*Revelation 6*
vs.4,5 False Christs	v.2 Man on a white horse
6 Wars and rumours	4 Man on a red horse
of wars	5 Man on a black horse
7 Famines	8 Man on a livid or green
7 Pestilences	horse
9 Persecutions	9 Souls of the martyrs
7 Earthquakes	12 A great earthquake

(It will be noticed that in Matthew's Gospel the earthquakes come in verse 7 after famines and pestilences, and before the martyrs and therefore out of the order of Revelation. Both Mark and Luke give the earthquakes before the famines and pestilences, and it is possible that during the whole period there will be a shaking of the whole structure of things, moral and administrative as well as physical, hence the different positioning.)

Unity of Prophecy

The seventh seal in Revelation is not opened until chapter 8 and it introduces a whole series of judgements from God called the seven trumpets and the seven vials, or bowls, and they lead right up to the coming of the Lord in glory in chapter 19. So in Matthew we have a whole series of sorrows also, culminating in verses 29 to 30, *Immediately after the tribulation of those days shall the sun be darkened....and then shall appear the sign of the Son of Man in heaven.*

The words of the Lord Himself in Matthew 24 firmly link the events of Daniel on the one hand with those of Revelation on the other, and this puts us on firm ground in our line of interpretation. There are also other links in the New Testament, for in 2 Thessalonians 2.4 we find *the man of sin....sitting in the Temple of God, showing himself that he is God.*

And again in Revelation 13.14 the False Prophet causes a speaking and moving image of the Beast to be made and set up for worship in the stead of God. All who refuse to accept his mark and submit to him as God he turns on with fury, and since he controls all means of coercion this means tribulation, and Revelation makes it clear that it is *the Great Tribulation.*

So again we are assured that the plan is one and fits together in all its parts both in the Old and New Testaments. This, in turn, leads into our next study, which concerns these coming world rulers and their places in the program of God.

Coming World Rulers - Civil and Religious

5

Each of our studies thus far has taken us to a point where human world rule reaches its terminus and is destroyed by God at the appearing of the Lord Jesus Christ in glory. Through centuries of the development of man's schemes for a world of his own choice we have seen him at the end of each chapter lined up under his leaders in open rebellion *against the Lord and His anointed.* Many Scriptures describe this final revolt of man, among them Psalm 2; Zechariah 14.2,3; Dan. 7.24-27; Ezek. 38; 2 Thess. 2.3-8; Rev. 19.11-21 etc.

Each prophetic portion studied has brought us to ten kings, later dominated by one who overshadows the whole scene. Others yield and submit to him, and he presses forward, not only for world dominion, but to set himself up in the place of God. This is the culmination of humanism - the enthronement and deification of man, the very foundation of most non-Christian thinking in our own days. The movement has been marked and deliberate from the time of the renaissance onward.

But in Revelation 13 we have seen that there are two beasts, each representing a distinct world leader. In the same book, chapters 17-18, we have another leader robed in scarlet, who is called a prostitute and who is riding the political beast. In Daniel 11 and 12, as well as Ezekiel 38, and many other passages we have other kings mentioned as connected with the events of the last days. Some of these we have glanced at in passing, but must now consider in more detail. They are all of interest and even though there are areas

34

where opinions differ as to details of interpretation, and where there is much that is not clearly revealed or defined by God, there is still a great deal that is important for the completion of the picture and for the understanding of God's plans. To these we now turn.

Rome revived

The ten kings with whom so many of the passages of Daniel end, as well as Revelation 17, are in the fourth of the world empires, the final form of that which followed Greek rule. This can only be the Roman Empire since it was the conqueror and absorber of Alexander's domain, as well as being the power under which Messiah died, and whose people destroyed Jerusalem, Dan. 9.26.

Since Rome has never at any time in the past existed as a ten kingdom federation this must refer to a future phase; a fact which is further confirmed by seeing that *in the days of those kings* and following their destruction *God will set up a kingdom that shall never be destroyed.* In other words Messiah's Millennial reign will begin immediately following the removal of this last Gentile empire, something which, in the very nature of things obviously must be still future.

It is clear, however, that among these ten kings one will emerge as the super-dictator of the last days, and since he is by far the most prominent and important human figure on the world scene we must study more closely what Scripture has to say about him.

Arnold Toynbee in his "Study of History" insists that though the Roman Empire broke up as a political entity it continued to exist as a cultural one through its many parts. He points out that no new civilization arose to take its place, but that its laws, administrative structures, political philosophies, and even its speech through the Latin basis, live on in the European nations which to this day are merely a projection of the Roman culture.

Scripture leads us to expect a revival or restoration of some form of that Roman structure. Today we see the very nations that represent this and occupy its territory striving to build and maintain a European Economic Community shortly to embrace ten nations, and based on an agreement called "The Treaty of Rome." It no longer seems such a farfetched idea. Just as *Zionism* gained momentum, and Israel, after long ages of dispersion and "Not-a-people" status, suddenly became a major factor in world affairs, so her opposite number in the great drama of the future began to take shape in the development of *Europism*.

The first beast

This future super-dictator appears in Scripture under a number of names: *The prince that shall come*, Dan.9.26; *The Beast*, Rev.13.1; 19.19; *The man of sin, The wicked one, The son of perdition*, 2 Thess.2.3-8.

Under threat and pressure from the Kings of the North and the South, to be referred to later, Dan.11.40, Israel makes a defensive treaty with this head of the Western or European Empire, Dan.9.27, but it will be *a covenant with death, and an agreement with hell*, Isa.28.15, and though made for *one week* of seven years it will be violated by the Beast in the middle of the week, Dan.9.27, by causing the sacrifice to cease and by setting up the desolating abomination, Dan.12.11. This abomination is said by the Lord Jesus to *stand in the sanctuary*, Matt.24.15. In 2 Thessalonians 2.4 we read that the Man of Sin *will sit in the Temple of God showing himself that he is God*. Revelation 13.14-15 indicates that it will actually be some kind of working and speaking image of him that will be there and be worshipped by those who bow and take his mark.

Opposition to this attempted usurpation of the prerogatives of God, and the demand that worship which belongs exclusively to God be given to him, will signal the beginning of the greatest pogrom and the most intense period of human suffering ever experienced on earth. It is *the tribulation the great one*, Matt.24.15-22. So in Daniel 11.35-38 the Wilful King is said to *exalt himself against every god and speak marvellous things against the God of gods....neither shall he regard the God of his fathers.* In Daniel 7.25 he *speaks great words against the Most High, and wears out the saints of the Most High.* In Revelation 13.5,7 he has *a mouth speaking great blasphemies....and he makes war with the saints.*

He is Devil-inspired, coming out of the bottomless pit as to his origin, Rev.17.8, and has all the power and authority of Satan as well as his throne, Rev.13.8. That is, of course, the throne of the nations which Satan offered to the Lord in Luke 4, which offer was summarily rejected. He leads his subordinate but confederated co-rulers in *war against the Lamb,* Rev.17.14; 19.19, but is finally overthrown and destroyed in the Lake of Fire at the coming in glory of the Lord Jesus Christ, Dan.7.26; 9.27; 11.45; 2 Thess.2.8; Rev.19.20.

In 2 Thessalonians 2.9 we are told that, as a result of his league with Satan he has miraculous powers and performs *acts of power, signs, and* lying *wonders.* It should be noted that the identical three Greek words are used in Acts 2.22 of the sign-miracles of the Lord Jesus which He performed to authenticate the genuineness of His Messiahship. They are also used in 2 Corinthians 12.12 of the authenticating signs performed by the Apostles sent out by the Lord. Miracles of the same kind will be performed by Satan's minion in those terrible days but they are branded as *lying,* i.e., spurious, deceptive, and the opposite of genuine.

In spite of his control of virtually all means of communication, all administrative authority, all economic power and all religious influence so that anyone resisting his absolute dominion can be made a non-person unable to buy or sell and therefore unable to live, he will yet be cut down, coming to a sudden end, and *none shall help him,* Dan.11.45.

The False Prophet

There are some similarities between this Devil-inspired and probably demon possessed pair, yet there are many distinctions which must be clearly marked if we are to understand their relative positions, and where they fit into the general picture.

1) The first beast demands and assumes supreme power. The second (false prophet) takes a position under the first and works only for his advancement.

2) The first is a Gentile; rises out of *the sea* with his throne in Rome, *the seven hilled city* of Revelation 17.9. The second is a Jew, *out of the land* with his seat in Jerusalem where he erects the image of the first in the Temple.

3) The first is a secular head, with governmental power. The second is a religious leader (a prophet) with miraculous spirit powers, Rev. 13.14,15.

4) The first demands worship as God. The second promotes and compels the worship of the first.

5) Both have Satanic motivation, the second, however, operates with delegated authority. While it is not specifically stated in Scripture it seems probable that it is the False Prophet who in Palestine urges and promotes Israel's alliance with the Beast in the first place, just as other false prophets in the Old Testament did, leading the nation into disastrous leagues with God's enemies for which the nation suffered in the end.

Thus we see in Revelation 16.13-14 opposed to the Holy and Benign Trinity of the heavens, Father, Son, and Holy Spirit each functioning in His proper relationship and sphere, there is a triumvirate of evil and malignity from the pit - Satan, the Beast, and the False Prophet. Each is striving for control of men, spirit, soul, and body - the one for blessing, the other for eternal destruction.

In Revelation 19.20 the False Prophet shares the doom of his leader when both are cast alive into the Lake of Fire.

The King of the North

Israel's most feared and unrelenting foes of antiquity came from the north, and the books of the prophets have many ominous references to these foes as the instruments of God's anger *from the north.* Isaiah 14.31 speaks of a dark cloud of Divine retribution coming like *smoke from the north.* In 41.25 the same prophet says, *I have raised up one from the north....he shall come upon princes....as the potter treadeth clay.* Jeremiah 1.15 says, *I will call all the families of the kingdoms of the north, saith the Lord; and they shall come and set up every one his throne at the entering in of the gates of Jerusalem... and against all the cities of Judah.* In some passages this enemy from the north is simply called *the Assyrian* or *the king of Assyria,* as in Isaiah 7.17 and this is also the very passage in which deliverance is linked with the sign of the virgin-born son who would be called IMMANUEL.

Many prophetic passages of the Bible, perhaps most of them, have a primary and local fulfilment, and this partial fulfilment of these passages is now, of course, a matter of history. We know that Assyria carried the ten northern tribes off into exile more than 130 years before Nebuchadnezzar destroyed Jerusalem and deported the people of Judah to Babylon. But it is also very clear that behind the prophecies of these kings and armies of the north lurked allusions to a more deadly foe of the end times, sometimes foreshadowed directly by these very northern oppressors. In order to understand clearly the origin of the theme of the King of the North we must return to Daniel, and go back a bit on the scroll not only of prophecy but also of history.

Origins of the Kings of North and South

In Daniel 8 a separate little prophetic history of Medo-Persia and Greece is given, in which we see that Alexander the Great, the great horn of the he-goat, would be broken off and four horns would grow to take his place. And so it happened, for as we have already seen, when Alexander died the Greek Empire was divided between his four generals who became, respectively, the kings of the North, South, East and West.

Ptolemy Soter took Egypt and was called *King of the South,* of which more later. Seleucus grabbed Babylonia, Cappadocia, Phrygia, Upper Syria, and Mesopotamia, later adding many countries so that, by the time of his death by assassination in 281 B.C., he ruled an empire stretching from the Punjab in India to the western shores of Turkey. This is the founder of the royal house of the Seleucidae - Kings of the North.

Of this kingdom sprang *the king of a fierce, or brazen, countenance* of Daniel 8.23, the infamous Antiochus Epiphanes, one of Israel's most relentless persecutors and enemies who, in his frenzied hatred of Israel and her God desolated the sanctuary by sacrificing a sow on the great altar of the Temple. But the fact that this vision was to be shut up, v.26, because it was *for many days,* that is, far in the future, hints that Antiochus was merely the foreshadowing of an even more sinister and brutal personality of the end times.

Chapter 11 of Daniel is really a projection of chapter 8, going into more detail and carrying the story right down to the end times. Chapter 8 left off at the overthrow of the then existing Persian Empire but adding some events of the later development of one of the parts of the succeeding Greek dominion. Then in 10.14 the thread is taken up again by Daniel's celestial visitor who says, *I am come to make thee understand what shall befall thy people in the latter days.* This is really the introduction to chapter 11 which bears directly on the future kings of north and south so important to our present study.

Dr. F. A. Tatford in his book "The Climax of the Ages" says, "This chapter is concerned primarily with the intrigues, alliances, and conflicts of the kings of the north and the south from the times of Cyrus of Persia to the setting up of the Millennial Kingdom." A large part of this has already been fulfilled historically and details may be found in Dr. Tatford's book, pages 189-211, with which we are not at the moment directly concerned. Our interest lies in the fact that in this chapter we have such specific references to major powers and kings *of the end times,* and that they are linked with the Beast, or head of the revived Roman Empire, in the final act of the great drama of world history.

"The King"

Following a rapid sketch of Antiochus Epiphanes and his activities in chapter 11 there comes an abrupt change at verse 35 with the words, *Some of those who have insight will fall in order to refine, purge, and make them pure, UNTIL THE END TIME, BECAUSE IT IS STILL TO COME AT THE AP- POINTED TIME.* From here on there appears a character simply called "the King," obviously at the end times referred to, but about whom there has been much discussion almost as fruitless as it has been endless. Some believe he is the Beast or head of the Western Empire; some that he is a renegade and apostate ruler of Israel. He cannot be the King of the North, nor yet of the South since these are said to *push at him* and *come against him* in verse 40. The reference to his entering in- to the countries, overflowing and passing over, and entering into the glorious land (surely the land of Israel) etc. makes it difficult to see how he could be king of Israel, despite the revered names advocating the theory. The only figure big enough and fitting the description is the dictator of the Roman Empire.

Self-willed, magnifying himself above all gods (see 2 Thess.2.4), speaking marvellous things against the God of gods (see Dan.7.25), honouring the god of forces and so on, he is the great antagonist of God Himself. About the only reason advanced for seeing in him an apostate Jewish leader is the phrase *Neither shall he regard the God* (or gods) *of his fathers,* Dan.11.37, this being taken as a peculiarly Jewish expression because sometimes used by Jews. But Romans and Greeks and other pagans also used the term "god of his fathers" as do many peoples to this day, and the argument hardly seems a very strong or valid one.

But whoever this king may be, our main concern at the moment is not so much with him as with his attackers: the King of the North and the King of the South, 11.40, for they are the last and final descendants of a long line bearing these titles. Obviously the King of the North is to be identified with the great northern confederacy which suffers such an awe- some defeat in Ezekiel 38 and 39 and who is said to *come up from the north parts,* 39.2.

Now compare Ezekiel 38.2,5,6 with Genesis 10.2 and note the names Gog, Magog, Rosh, Gomer, Tubal, and Meshech. Authorities have concluded that here we have what the ancients called the Scythians, who lived in the area of the Caucasus, Black Sea and Caspian Sea; in other words Russia and the countries under her control. This power will also have under her control, according to Ezekiel 38.5, Persia, Ethiopia (not of N.E. Africa but "Cush", a name at that time of N. Arabia), Libya, but again not of No. Africa since the name "Put" refers to the land of that name close to Iran or Persia. Next we have Gomer, referred to in the Jewish Talmud as the Germani or Germans. The fifth ally of the King of the North is Togarmah, now generally identified by scholars as the ancient name of Turkey and Armenia. A formidable host indeed, and such is the King of the North, one of Israel's deadliest foes in the final struggle - the great northern confederacy, headed by Russia.

The King of the South

This title in the Old Testament has always referred to Egypt and her ruler, the ancient enslaver where Israel faced extinction under the genocidal fury of the Pharaohs. Later on Egypt passed under the heel of different world powers, and was finally completely subjugated by Alexander, only to be taken over by the Ptolemaic dynasty, of whom, by the way, Cleopatra was descended and like all the rest ruled Egypt with not a drop of Egyptian blood in her veins.

At the end time it is probable that the King of the South will represent not only Egypt but also the whole Pan-African or perhaps Arab-Moslem league to the leadership of which she has long aspired. It would also seem from Daniel 11.40 that the King of the South will be in league with, if not allied to, the King of the North in their opposition to the growing power and megalomania of the Beast at the head of the Western Empire. As it is today they are seen in various states of collusion or alliance, yet always eyeing each other with suspicion and distrust, and ready to jump on each other when it suits their purposes. The focus of all their attention is Palestine, and like a magnet it draws them on. The Beast of the West is tied to Israel by a treaty confirmed for one week of seven years and is therefore bound to defend her from her two enemies of North and South. At this critical juncture, see

Revelation 16.12, God removes the barrier holding back another force.

The Kings of the East

This clearing of the way for the armies beyond the Euphrates is said in Revelation 16.12 (see also 9.15) to be an act of God to gather all the kings of the earth to His own trysting place so that He can deal with them. In Revelation 16.13-14 the gathering is said to be the result of demonic deception; in 19.19 they gather voluntarily; while Zechariah 14.1-2 says specifically that, whoever the instruments may be, it forms part of God's sovereign plan to gather them there around Jerusalem. His purpose is to break Israel and bring her to repentance and restoration, and then to break and judge all these rebellious nations. These hordes of the Orient will sweep like a flood over a doomed western civilization rotten to the core and long ready for destruction. So we read that when *the King* is already tangled in a Palestine campaign and driving against the King of the South, *tidings out of the East and out of the North shall trouble him*, Dan.11.44, but *in the holy mountain* he comes to his end, dealt with by God, Dan.11.45.

The false church, allied to the political system

Linked to the Beast of the Western European Empire is another power which we must look at while studying world rulers of the end times, namely, the Scarlet Woman: the Harlot Church of Revelation 17 and 18.

That she represents a great world power or organization is clear from the words *sitting on many waters, with whom the kings of the earth have committed fornication, and the inhabitants of the earth have been made drunk...* , Rev.17.1,2. But she is evidently a religious or ecclesiastical power who, for a time at least, dominates and controls the Beast of political government, since she is seen riding on it. She is a counterfeit, a harlot, unfaithful and promiscuous, dabbling in world affairs for her own profit and aggrandizement, and masquerading in the place of the virgin Bride of Christ, the true Church of all believers. She is rich and influential,

Rev.17.4; 18.11-13. She represents a phase of world religion hitherto unrevealed, *a mystery*, Rev.17.5. She has been a persecutor of God's true children, Rev.17.6; 18.20. She will be destroyed by the political power she has for so long controlled and manipulated, before it, in turn, is destroyed by the coming of the Lord, that is, late in the tribulation period.

It seems that this great world system of religion can only be the World Church of the Ecumenical Movement, headed, of course, by the only world church system which has ever existed - that of Rome - but embracing all the apostate branches of Christendom. The first Christians were plainly told, *You are not of the world, just as I am not of the world,* and the church throughout the New Testament is presented as made up of those called *out of the world.* Yet before our very eyes today we see this mammoth humanistic structure taking form, with the denial of almost every basic doctrine of Holy Scripture, and at the moment working on the production of a "World Bible open to constant revision and change, and acceptable to all shades of thought within the Ecumenical Church."

The true Christian is called upon to *come out of her, my people, that ye be not partaker of her sins,* Rev.18.4. For the instructed Christian knows that, after the removal of the true Church at the Rapture, this false church will go marching on to her supreme moment of power, and also to her inevitable doom.

In view of the teaching of the Holy Scripture about Israel, the Beast, the False Prophet, the Kings of the North and of the South, the Harlot Church of Babylon, is it not startling that we have, either formed or in the process of formation, even today the Israeli nation, the Community of Europe, the Communist Confederacy, the Pan-African Community sponsored and led by Egypt, the Ecumenical Church, herself linked with a United Nations organization in which the very name of God and His Son are prohibited and never mentioned? All of these developments were unheard of 50 years ago, some of them a great deal less, and until recently were not even reckoned as of importance or to be more than the pipe dreams of idealists.

6 The Coming of the Lord to take the Church away

We have seen God following with precision His own timetables for Israel and also for the Gentile nations. Those timetables led us step by step to the first coming of Messiah and His *cutting off*, then on to the destruction of the Holy City by *the people of the prince that shall* (later) *come,* thus bringing us down to Titus and the year 70 A.D. God had waited, even after Calvary, looking for national repentance on the part of the Jews, but they stoned Stephen, rejected the preaching of *Jesus as the Christ* by the Apostles through the early part of the book of the Acts. Because of this the nation, as such, was set aside, Roms.11.15-20, veiled, 2 Cor.3.14, and blinded, Roms.11.10, while the Gospel went out to the whole lost world in a general amnesty to *whosoever will* on the basis of faith and not of race.

This salvation for Gentiles is the result of the fall of the Jews, Roms.11.11, and during the almost two thousand years of the Day of Grace, Israel's clock has been stopped, God's plans for her in abeyance, and her history *as a nation* suspended so far as God is concerned or His reckoning. During this long period God no longer *openly* intervenes in world affairs, but with His court of judgement in recess, meets men as a waiting Saviour. This age is not counted in Israel's history and therefore has no place in the above timetables, not once appearing directly in the revelations of the prophets. It is the time of the Bride of the Lamb; not the Wife of

Jehovah. It belongs to the Church in grace while she is His witness and representative during the long dark night of Israel's rejection and scattering. Sixty-nine of the weeks of years predicted in Daniel 9 are fulfilled up to the destruction of Jerusalem; the 70th and final week of seven years still lies ahead, awaiting the end of the age of grace and the removal of the Church to start *Operation Israel* again.

Indeed we are told in 2 Thessalonians 2.3 that the Day of the Lord which will include the judgements and the restoration of Israel cannot begin until the turning away, or apostasy, and the Man of Sin appear. The passage then goes on to say that this cannot take place until *that which withholds* and *He who restrains* are taken out of the way. We take these two to be the Church and the Holy Spirit who indwells the Church so as long as the Church remains on earth the last, doom-laden years of Israel's history prior to the Millennium cannot even begin.

Confirming this we find that in Revelation the Church is never seen after chapter 3, which ends the letters to the churches with the words, *Behold I come quickly,* 3.11, until she is seen *leaving heaven* with her Lord and Bridegroom to come back to earth for the setting up of the kingdom in 19.7-14. Instead of the Church we see God's witnesses on earth during that period of judgement to be 144,000 Israelites and we may safely conclude that were the Church on earth these witnesses would not be needed, Rev. 7.3-8. The only "church" on earth during all that time is the apostate world-church, the Harlot of chapters 17 and 18, who, of course, did not go when the believers were taken.

The Rapture

These facts would prepare us to look in Scripture for indications that, when the time comes for God to take up His ancient people He will remove His Church, and with it the only restraining influence in the world. In this we are not disappointed. There are a number of specific references:

1) John 14. The Lord Himself said, *If I go away I will come again and receive you unto myself.* In Matthew 24.30

He had already told His disciples of *the sign of the Son of Man coming or appearing in the heavens, with all tribes mourning as they see Him coming in power and great glory.* The reason for this reaction is given in 25.31-46, for it is a coming in judgement to set up His kingdom after calling all rebels to account and dismissing them to *everlasting punishment.* Compare Revelation 19. In John 14 all is so different. Here there is no wrath, no punishment, no horrified nations, no power and great glory or flaming fire, but simply, *I am coming again to receive you to myself.*

2) In 1 Thessalonians 4.16, written some 20 years after those words of the Lord were spoken, the Holy Spirit through the Apostle Paul fills in more detail regarding this great hope of the Church.

Paul had evidently taught the Christians at the time of their conversion about Christ's coming in glory to set up His kingdom and also about their share in it, 2 Thess. 2.5. In the meantime some had died, possibly through persecution, 1 Thess. 1.6; 4.14, and the survivors were troubled lest such might have lost their place in that kingdom, since they would not be on earth when Christ came to set it up. This misunderstanding Paul sets himself to correct. He first of all writes in verses 13 and 14 of 1 Thessalonians 4 that there was no need to be sad like those who have no hope because Christ and His Church are one body, His resurrection is theirs also, and the dead *must* be raised. Those who have died must be raised for another reason, because even *those who sleep in Jesus God will bring with Him,* i.e. when He comes to set up the kingdom He will bring them back to earth with Him. "But," the Thessalonians might have argued, "how can He bring them back from Heaven to Earth with Him if they are dead and buried in the earth, as we know only too well?" The answer to this comes in verses 15 to 18.

The opening sentence, *We say to you by the word of the Lord* cannot refer to already existing Scripture, since no such revelation is found in them up to this point. There is also no definite article before *word,* and W. E. Vine and others point out that it could, and possibly should be translated *in a word from the Lord*, referring to a special revelation of these further details given to Paul who is the only New Testament writer dealing with the Rapture.

Paul links himself with those who might be alive at the Rapture. There is no time set for this event and it has been, as it was intended to be, an ever present hope for God's children. No mention is ever made in Scripture of anything which must be fulfilled before it can take place, as is the case with the coming in glory and judgement, Matt. 24.

The living will have no advantage over the dead, as these Christians feared; indeed the dead are raised first. They are all His, dead and living alike, Rom. 14.9, and no part of His body can be left behind, as some would have us believe, leaving Christ with an incomplete body. The following chapter of 1 Thessalonians, 5.9-10 tells us specifically that *God has not destined us to wrath* (that is the coming wrath on earth spoken of in verse 3), *but for obtaining salvation through our Lord Jesus Christ, who died for us, that whether we are awake or asleep, we may live together with Him.*

The shout emphasizes His eagerness and desire to have His people with Him, as well as His rallying command which neither Satan nor the grave can hinder or thwart. Dead and living are caught up together "in clouds" to meet the Lord in the air, for He does not at this point come to earth at all. He will come to earth later, as recorded in Matt. 25.31,32; Zech. 14.4; Rev. 19.19, 20, etc.; at that time, *with* His saints. It is important to note in passing that when He appears in glory His people are always said to appear with Him coming from Heaven to earth and therefore must have been previously taken up. See Dan. 7.22,27; Col. 3.4; Rev. 19.14; Jude 14 etc.

3) 1 Corinthians 15.51, the other major New Testament passage on the Rapture, adds the following details:

a. What he now tells them was a mystery, that is, something not previously revealed, v.51.

b. It will take place suddenly and instantaneously, v.52.

c. At that time dead and living will be transformed. The dead, gone to corruption, will put on incorruptibility. The living who, though not gone to corruption are nonetheless mortal or subject to dying, will put on immortality. See 1 John 3.2 where we are told that *we shall be like Him for we shall see Him as He is.* See also Romans 8.29.

d. For the believer personally this is the consummation - to be not only delivered from the power and presence of physical death, but to be transformed into the very image of Christ. It is the moment of triumph, vs.55-57.

In a later chapter we shall be dealing with the coming of Christ *to* the earth in glory for the kingdom, and will, at that time, go into the Scriptural differences between the two stages of the coming and their distinctness. It is hard to understand how anyone reading carefully the Word of God would confuse the two or see them as the same. We might in the meantime consider the following list of distinctions and contrasts between the coming *for* the Christians and the coming *with* them.

The Rapture	*The Appearing*
Comes to the air.	Comes to earth.
To remove believers.	With believers to judge the world.
Imminent.	
Opens the way for the Man of Sin.	Preceded by signs.
	Dooms the Man of Sin.
Clears stage for the Tribulation.	Ends the Tribulation.
For comfort.	For judgement.
A "Mystery" only revealed in New Testament.	Revealed throughout Old Testament also.
Brings age of grace to an end.	Brings in Kingdom age.
Connected with program for Church,	with that of Israel and world.
Creation is left untouched.	Creation is renewed.
Believers' works reviewed for reward.	Nations judged for rebellion.

Final
Convulsions of 7
a Dying World

Having carried our studies through the period of the Christians' removal from earth, and the rise of the different world rulers after that happens, we must now take a look at the period called in the Bible *The Great Tribulation,* trying to trace the developments of that last tumultuous phase of our present world history.

The reader must keep in mind that while we refer to the whole calamitous period as The Great Tribulation it is actually composed of a number of different streams converging at that time.

1) *It is the accumulated harvest of man's mad sowing through the course of many centuries.* Man has tolerated corruption in politics, often because he shared the benefits of it, he has encouraged violence in the name of liberty, he has paid men to carry out the perversion of our institutions of learning in the name of intellectual emancipation, he has connived at the prostitution of justice, and smiled at increasing permissiveness in every phase of our society, he has bowed tamely to lawless minority pressures etc. These paths have led and will lead to violence among nations, wars, famines, pestilences, and persecutions which are *the beginning of sorrows* and which prepare the stage for the coming of the Tribulation itself.

2) *It is the final outburst of Satan's malignant hatred against Israel* as the channel of blessing for the world through Messiah. Since he has failed to destroy or thwart Christ

Himself he turns in fury on the remnant of Israel's seed, Rev. 12.13-17 with all of chapter 13.

3) *It is the Beast's persecution of all those who refuse to take his mark or to give him worship, Rev. 13.7,15,16.*

4) *It is the product of the greed and unbridled power-hunger of the great political blocs of the world,* focussed in the Near East, Zech. 14.1-3.

5) *It is God's punishment on the godless nations* for their rebellion against Him: the end of the road that began with the rejection of His Son, Rev. 8.13-9.21.

6) *But above all, it is the TIME OF JACOB'S TROUBLE, Jer. 30.7,* when God will deal with His wayward people in judgement to bring them to repentance and ultimate blessing.

Since it would be impossible in this brief and simple study to go into a detailed study of these separate ingredients that go to make up *the wine of the wrath of God, poured out in full strength in the cup of His indignation,* we must content ourselves by following the broad outlines of its course as given to us in Revelation chapters 6-18. To do so intelligently, however, we must go back again for a moment to Daniel, chapter 9, to remind ourselves of one or two important points, for that passage is one of the main hinges and pivots of all prophecy, both in the Old Testament and the New Testament.

The Abomination

Daniel tells us that because of pressure from the kings of the North and South, Israel will appeal to the head of the European Federation (the revived Roman Empire) for help, and will for this purpose make a treaty or pact with him for a period of one week of years. See page 36. This is that 70th and final week which will bring Israel's earthly history to consummation.

The pact is confirmed, but in the middle of the week the Beast violates it by causing the sacrifices to cease in the Temple. We learn from Daniel 12.11 that this suspension of worship is because *the abomination that causes desolation* is set up in the sanctuary. This setting up of a desolating symbol of idolatry is mentioned in Matthew 24.15,21 as that which sets off the Great Tribulation. In 2 Thessalonians 2.4 we are told that this blasphemous antagonist of God and His people will not only oppose God but will *sit in the Temple of God showing himself that HE is God.* From Revelation 13.14-18 we further learn that it is really an image of the Beast which the False Prophet sets up, one so real that it at least appears to be alive and actually speaks. The Beast himself will be ruling from Rome and not Jerusalem.

Divine worship is claimed for this abomination and he whom it represents, and those who bow to him must receive his mark, that mysterious symbol of the deification of man which Satan had promised him in Eden if he would only refuse obedience to God - *Ye shall be as gods,* Gen.3. The mark of the Beast is 666; the fulness of all that man can be or achieve, as seven is the number of the fulness of God so prominent in this book of symbols - The Apocalypse.

So the Beast will demand from all in general but from Israel in particular his awesome price for the promised aid. God, however, will have His witnesses on earth even in those fearsome times, as we shall see in our next study, and those who have accepted their message from God will refuse the mark of the Beast and deny him their worship. This explains the substance of the everlasting Gospel in chapter 14, verses 6 and 7, *Fear God, give glory to Him .... and worship Him... .* The basic and acid test of everyone then as now is simply who and what he worships. The Beast will then set about the persecution and extermination with fire and sword, and so dreadful will those days be that if God did not shorten them His people would be completely wiped out, Matt.24.22.

We know from Daniel that this violation will take place *in the middle of the week* and the Tribulation in the true sense begins from that point. But what of the first half of the seven year period? Scripture has much to say about it, and although not approaching the Tribulation in severity it will still be a time of mounting horror and suffering. The difference seems to be that during the first half of the seven years man will be reaping what he has sown, paying the price for his own folly and wickedness without direct and open intervention by God, whereas during the second half God will step in, will summon direct punishment through the instrumentality of men, demons, and angels. The most detailed description is, of course, in Revelation, chapters 5-19, all of which falls under the heading of *things which shall be after these things,* Rev.1.19.

It will help to understand this whole book if the reader recognizes that the entire chronological forward-moving part of the Revelation is contained in the sections giving the Seven Seals, chapter 6, the Seven Trumpets, chapters 8 and 9, and the Seven Vials or Bowls, chapter 16. Most of the other material in the book is either close-up sketches of the leading personalities in the drama, celestial, terrestrial, or infernal; or else instruction as to the origins of the action as from these three sources.

The Seven Seals

Each one of the three groups of seven sorrows gains in intensity over the preceding group, but there are other differences as well which will appear as we proceed.

In the seals we see first *a white horse* with his crowned rider going out to bring men under his sway, and in the parallel portion in Matthew 24.5 the Lord warned of *many* (false Christs) *coming in my name saying, 'I am the Christ' and shall deceive many.*

Next comes *a red horse* whose rider has power to take peace from the earth and set men to killing one another. The explanation in Matthew 24.6 is, *Ye shall hear of wars and rumours of wars.*

Then appears *a black horse* whose rider carries a weighing scale and proclaims food at inflationary famine prices. A denarius (penny) was a day's wages, Matt.20.2, and a "choenix" (measure) of wheat or oats was a slave's ration, yet it is now selling for more than eight times its normal price. So in Matthew 24.7 famine follows war, as indeed it always does.

Just as famine follows war, so on the heels of famine we have pestilences, or diseases on a sweeping epidemic scale,

Matt.24.7. This answers to the fourth seal and its "pale" or *livid green horse* and rider; the sickly hue of pestilence and rotting bodies.

The fifth seal shows the souls of martyrs under the altar awaiting the just vengeance of God on their killers, and in the Matthew passage the first four movements only introduced a period when those faithful to the true Christ will be *delivered up to be tortured and killed and hated by all nations for my name's sake,* 24.9.

Seal number six brings the earthquake mentioned in Matthew 24.7. It will be noticed that there is an inversion of the order of five and six in Matthew and Revelation. But the order of the earthquakes in the different Gospels giving this material is also different, and it is highly possible that earthquakes will occur *throughout* this whole tumultuous period, winding up with one great earth-shaking as in Revelation 6.12.

These earthquakes may be understood literally with attendant phenomena in the heavens, or symbolically of the shaking of the very foundations of social life and government in the world with the collapse of all administration and authority at every level. Sun, moon, and stars in Scripture often stand for central, derived, and local rule. The interpretation has long been debated, but we see no reason why both should not be true, the literal merely illustrating and reflecting in the physical heavens what is taking place morally in the affairs of men. Not merely sun, moon, and stars, but mountains and islands, kings and nobles - all is in chaos and dissolution. Nothing stands; nothing is stable; all has reverted to the jungle, and men are back skulking in caves and dens trying to hide from the reality of the face and presence of God.

The seventh seal, at Revelation 8.1, simply allows the scroll to open all the way to the end of the drama, and it therefore includes everything from this shaking of heaven and earth to the final crisis. The first part of the unfolding is in the form of seven angelic trumpet blasts, each one bringing a new sharp blow of divine retribution on the rebellious earth. The seals showed us man reaping the harvest of his own folly, sin, and lawlessness in convulsions of false leaders, wars, famines, diseases, persecutions, pogroms, and upheavals both physical and spiritual which destroy every kind of security and order. In the trumpets the intervention of God from heaven is more direct and obvious.

The Seven Trumpets

At the *first trumpet*, 8.7, comes a sharp and intense outpouring of punishment from above onto the earth, scorching everything green and living. As well as environmental destruction, trees and grass may also refer to men, high and low as in Daniel 4.20-22 and 1 Peter 1.24. The reference to one third of trees and grass being affected in these trumpet judgements possibly indicates that they fall mainly on the Western or European Empire of the Beast at this time.

The *second trumpet* describes a great flaming mountain or volcano bringing death to the same area of the Empire. In Jeremiah 51.25 Babylon is referred to as a destroying mountain, while in Daniel 2.34,35 Christ's coming kingdom is likened to a *stone cut without hands* which demolishes the whole structure of corrupted world rule and then grows *until it becomes a great mountain filling the whole earth.* So this volcanic mountain is probably some new form of world government (that of the Beast?) bringing with it throughout the Western Empire death and destruction.

The *third trumpet* brings a great star called Wormwood, its fall from the heavens possibly indicating some apostate religious leader who, flaming in bitterness, will poison the rivers and fountains or sources of instruction. This evil influence on the moral and ecclesiastical level will pollute and corrupt morals, principles, and motives throughout the west on a scale hitherto unimagined, and with the corruption will come moral death.

The *fourth trumpet*, 8.12, following this corruption of the very sources of public life, brings in the undermining and collapse of all rule and administrative authority. The sun, speaking of central rule; the moon, delegated or reflected rule; the stars, local administration - all breaks down, Gen.

1.18. This could be, as suggested by A.C.Gaebelein, "a mighty political convulsion in which all authority is subverted, from the despotic head to the petty magistrate of the town, on the pattern of atheistic, anarchical communism." We have had many examples in our days of how quickly a whole political system can be subverted.

The *fifth trumpet* is blown in 9.1 and a star fallen from heaven, either Satan himself, the fallen head of angels, Is.14.12-17, or his delegate on earth, opens the abyss and unleashes hordes of hitherto imprisoned evil spirits, otherwise known as demons. These overshadow the whole earth with a pall of darkness like dense smoke, and in this darkness these spirit powers, are now at last turned loose on a doomed world, a world which has for so long sought after and played with such things, during the time that true Christians were locked in constant battle with them, Eph.6.11-18. These are as unlimited in number as endless clouds of locusts, but unlike locusts which are harmless to humans, these are as vicious in their nature as scorpions. Those not sealed for God alone are their target, and so great is the distress that men long for relief in death and are denied any such escape.

It is a planned campaign, for they have a king who leads them, called in Hebrew and Greek *The Destroyer,* v.11, and they themselves are said to be in battle order, v.7. They have authority (crowns), intelligence (faces of men), seductive appeal (the hair of women), irresistible destructiveness (teeth of lions).

What a picture of the writhings of western civilization! It is now darkened, misled by false religious leaders, its governments reeling and useless, its leaders and nobles hiding in dens and caves, and now overwhelmed by unnumbered waves of evil spirits released from the pit by Satan or his representative, under permission from God to punish those who are in revolt against Him!

The *sixth trumpet,* 9.13, releases four angels at the River Euphrates who have, up to this point, been restrained. These may represent fallen angels and their work of stirring vast numbers of invading foes from the Orient. Again we feel that whatever literal and human enemies may be in view, there are yet behind them hordes of malignant spirits from that part of the world long identified as the home of the occult. This is indicated in verses 20-21 by their *demon worship, idolatry, murders, sorceries, fornication, and theft.* It is also not without significance that the Greek word used here and translated *sorceries* is *pharmakos* from which we get pharmacy and pharmaceutics, and refers to spells, enchantments, and witchcraft cast by means of potions, drugs, or medicines.

The *seventh trumpet* simply introduces the pouring out of

The Seven Vials or Bowls

These seven are a detailed breakdown of the direct judgements of God poured out at the sounding of the seventh trumpet. They are a series of devastating strokes from God on an already tottering and grief-maddened world and bringing to its consummation God's justice on a rebellious race, Rev. 16.17. This really carries us right through to chapter 19 with the appearing of Christ to crush all His foes at Armageddon and set up His kingdom, since chapters 17 and 18 deal with the destruction of the false harlot church and that takes place toward the end of the Tribulation and just before the appearing. We notice briefly the outline of the judgements introduced by the seven bowls.

1) Physical affliction on those who accepted the mark of the Beast, 16.2; 13.16-17.

2) Death and corruption spreading over the very seas. Either literal pollution and death of the oceans, or of the masses of mankind of which the restless sea so often speaks.

3) Pollution, death, and corruption spreading up the rivers to the very sources of life itself.

4) Scorching heat from the sun, either literal and physical, or symbolic of blazing persecution from the central authority, or both.

5) The pressures of God's anger now zeroing in on the very throne of the Beast, causing suffering and sorrow on all men.

6) The last remaining barriers of restraint now removed from before great Oriental masses, so that the Mediterranean world is at last smothered in their armies. Evil spirits again in evidence, emanating from the triumvirate of evil: Satan, the Beast, and the False Prophet, who are fighting the purposes of the Holy Trinity for blessing.

In verse 15 *the coming* is mentioned since the demons have deluded the kings of the earth into a last desperate war against God and His people to set up their own empire of the earth, and they are gathered together at Armageddon for this purpose. We have already pointed out that while here the gathering is attributed to demons, and in chapter 19 they are said to gather of themselves, we are told in Zechariah 14.12 and other Scriptures that these are merely the instruments God uses to gather them there that He may deal with them in His own way.

And this is the sorry pass to which man has come with all his vaunted culture and scientific advances on the very eve of Christ's appearing in flaming fire to put an end to it all and introduce in its place that which He has had in mind all along but which man has rejected - *the Kingdom of God.*

God's Witnesses on Earth when the Church is gone

8

The Lord Jesus said in Matthew 24.14, *This Gospel of the Kingdom shall be preached in all the world for a witness to all nations, and then shall the end come.* A number of plain and simple truths are here spelled out in understandable terms.

1) God will have a witness on earth during the dreadful days He had just been describing; days of world confusion, persecution, and tribulation.

2) The witness will involve the preaching of *the Gospel of the Kingdom,* a sample of which we have in Matthew 3.2, *Repent for the kingdom of heaven is at hand.* This preparation for a kingdom about to be set up is, quite obviously, not the same as, *Believe on the Lord Jesus Christ and thou shalt be saved,* as even a cursory study of the subject will reveal.

3) It will be preached world wide, *to all nations.*

4) It will be preached right to *the end.*

5) This end is that enquired about by the disciples in Matthew 24.3, *The end of the age,* and clearly the age is brought to an end by *the coming of the Son of Man,* or Christ in Millennial glory.

Some people feel, as they read of this witness during the last seven years of Israel's sorrows in *the times of the*

Gentiles that it must be the witness of the church and that therefore the church must be on earth then. That this is not so is clearly shown by two simple facts:

1) The Gospel they preach is *not* that preached by the church in this age, and

2) The preachers are not the same either, for they are clearly stated in Revelation 7.1-8 to be all Jews with an equal number marked out from each tribe by God for the purpose, before a single sorrow of the Great Tribulation can begin. The very fact that before the Tribulation can begin God chooses *Jewish witnesses* for His work shows clearly that His chosen witnesses of our age are no longer on earth, and also that Israel is back again in centre stage with the message of God; a kingdom message suited to a special Jewish need and situation. Such a message is certainly not suited to the present age of grace when men are warned to *flee from the coming wrath* while then they will be in the midst of it. Indeed, as we have already pointed out, from the end of chapter 3 the only church seen on earth is the ecumenical harlot church of chapters 17 and 18 until we come to chapter 19 where the true church is seen coming down to earth *from heaven* where she has been all along so far as that book is concerned.

But how wonderful, and also how like God, that even in the time of judgement, in the days of the Beast He will continue His work of grace, and proclaim afresh His power to save. Perhaps there is no greater demonstration of the power of God than this, that He will have a witness in the time when His arch-enemy holds sway on earth through the Beast and the False Prophet, who between them will control all life and all means of communication and coercion so that only those who bow to them and receive the mark of the Beast will be able to exist. God will still have His men and women, faithful to Him in spite of every kind of suffering. His message will not only be preached, but will be so preached, and with such power from God, that multitudes will be saved.

The multitudes saved
during the Tribulation

Having shown John the Jewish witnesses of the tribulation period, and their sealing by God for their work, He proceeds to give him a preview of the results of their mission, and shows him *a great multitude which no man could number, out of all nations and kindreds, and peoples, and tongues .... before the Lamb clothed in white robes and with palms in their hands*, Rev.7.9. These are identified in verse 14 as *those who have come out of great tribulation* (lit. 'the tribulation, the great one') *and have washed their robes and made them white in the blood of the Lamb.* These can only be those converted to God through the preaching of the 144,000 witnesses and now at last they have triumphed (palms in their hands) and are beyond all suffering in the very presence of God. It should be emphasized from this last passage that whatever phase or aspect of the Gospel is preached, the foundation must always be *the blood of the Lamb.*

And how loudly this all speaks for God's grace and power in upholding His witnesses in such a time! We sometimes excuse ourselves for lack of faithfulness in working for Him by pointing out how "difficult" our particular situation may be in the home, the work, the school, or even the church. These Jewish witnesses courageously speak for Him when to do so means horrible retaliation and almost certain death, and yet God's word triumphs in its confrontation with the Beast and all his might.

We have a sidelight on this activity in Matthew 25.31-46. There we read that when the Lord comes back to earth and is enthroned, He gathers all the nations before Him. These are at that time divided into three groups; the receivers, the rejectors, and *these my brethren*. The brethren must be those of His own earthly race, the *witnesses* from among the Jews. The sheep are those who in receiving them received the One who sent them. The goats are those who in rejecting them reject their Sender. The first group, note well, go into *the kingdom prepared for you*. The rejectors, who chose the Beast and his mark rather than Christ and His salvation along with His suffering, are consigned to everlasting punishment.

The Jewish Remnant

Some people begin wondering at this point where such Jewish witnesses will come from; who they are; how they will come to know the Lord and His Messiah after the Church is gone and all genuine preaching has ceased. We do not know the answer to any of these questions, since God does not seem to have said anything about them apart from the facts we have mentioned. Where God has not spoken it is neither wise nor profitable to speculate.

There need be no difficulty in our minds, however, about any of these things. In recent years there has been a real groundswell of enquiry and concern among Jews, and particularly younger Jews, about the New Testament Scriptures and especially as to whether Jesus may not have been the Messiah after all. There have been large and agitated gatherings even in synagogues, to ask questions about whether or not they might have blundered into a ghastly mistake of murdering their rightful king, and be suffering for it now. Even the confusion of the Ecumenical world church may, under God, be contributing to this. Rabbis are mingling with Gentile church leaders and however unfaithful and even ignorant some of these may be, most of them probably not even Christians, the New Testament Scriptures *are* being read and circulated. Jews *are* being exposed to the historical facts of the rejection of Christ by the leaders of Israel, and there is a strong ferment working for a reconsideration of the whole matter.

As we have already seen, 2 Thessalonians 2.10-12 clearly teaches that no *Christ-rejector* of this age will have a second chance in the age to come, but will be deliberately given over by God to *believe the lie that they all might be judged.* But it is quite possible that many may have heard the Gospel at least vaguely without knowing enough to accept it, and yet not be classified as having deliberately rejected it. Or it may be that, having heard *of* the Gospel or the New Testament they will, under the shock of the sudden removal

of the Church, turn to the Scriptures themselves and be led
to Christ. The Holy Spirit has worked on numberless occasions
through the Word alone, and He can do so again. We have
even read that years ago a child of God, thinking of this need,
prepared New Testaments in Hebrew and Yiddish; packed
them in waterproof cases and stored them in and around the
rock city of Petra, for long ages now a dead ghost city. This
man believed that the Jews fleeing the massacres of the
Tribulation will find them there, and in their distress will read
them. The air is so dry there that nothing rots or decays.
Truly, "Omnipotence has servants everywhere."

The Scriptures are clear and impressive as to the hap-
penings of the last days - Messiah, the Beast, the False
Prophet, the King of the North, the King of the South, the
Desolating Abomination, etc., but *blindness in part has happened to Israel,* until the fulness of the Gentiles be come in,
Romans 11.25. We read again in 2 Corinthians 3.14-16, *Their
minds are blinded and until this day remains a veil untaken
away in the reading of the Old Testament. When Moses is
read the veil is upon their heart .... nevertheless when it* (the
heart of Israel) *shall turn to the Lord, the veil shall be taken
away.* So we believe that the blindness and veiling of mind
which God has sent to Israel for her sin will just as surely be
removed. Then, first of all in these witnesses and later in the
whole spiritual remnant of the nation, will come repentance
and turning to God, with its attendant salvation and national
restoration, Roms. 11.26,27.

Two witnesses

In Revelation 11.3-13 we are told of two special witnesses
sent by God at that time, i.e. in the last half of the seven year
period, and therefore in the Great Tribulation properly speaking. There has been much discussion and speculation about
these two, and sometimes heated arguments.

Some believe that these two are not to be taken literally,
even as to their number, but that they are representative of
"adequate testimony in the mouth of two or three witnesses." This, of course, may be so, though we see little reason

or justification for interpreting symbolically something which bears so easily a literal interpretation, and which is surrounded on every side by material which seems quite literal. We should consider the following:

They prophesy; they are clothed in sackcloth of mourning; their ministry is for 1260 days (at 360 days per lunar year this is the three and a half years of the Tribulation so often spoken of and indeed given in verse 2 as 42 months); when their work is completed they are killed by the Beast; lie unburied in the streets for three and a half days while their enemies rejoice; then in full view of everyone they are raised to life and taken up bodily in a cloud to heaven. All of this seems to us to ring with the tone of literalness, and so we accept it.

Along with their other functions they perform miracles, all of them miracles of judgement against those who would withstand or attack them. They do not go out of their way to destroy anyone. The miracles seem to be purely defensive, in order to preserve them alive, and from this we gather that by this time the persecution has become so savage and complete that only by this means can God maintain a witness for Himself at all, at least in Jerusalem. By this time perhaps even the 144,000 witnesses are being almost if not altogether liquidated, and these two prophet-witnesses with power to defend themselves by fire and plague are necessary in Jerusalem. At their removal a severe earthquake shakes the Jewish capital causing 7,000 deaths and forcing men to recognize *the God of Heaven.*

It is interesting to note that the two witnesses in verse 4 are said to stand in witness before *the God of the earth.* God is now laying claim to His creation while men recognize the Beast as lord of the earth. But men repudiate anything outside earth and murder His witnesses. So they are then forced to acknowledge that the God of the earth is one who is also the God of heaven.

At this moment all heaven shouts that *the kingdoms of this world are become the kingdoms of our Lord and of His Christ, and He shall reign for ever and ever,* for now we are in the last moments of the conflict and the end is in sight.

Chapters 12 to 15 are taken up with descriptions of the chief actors in the closing drama and of their plans and destiny. Chapters 17 and 18 give us the portrait of the harlot church and her destruction, so that there is only chapter 16 which gives any forward movement, and this is taken up with the sharp, final outpourings of God's anger before Christ actually comes in glory to reign.

So we see that from *before the Great Tribulation* and to its very end God will have and maintain perfect and complete witness for Himself on earth even when rebellion is at its worst. We also see that as a result of that testimony and through the blood of the Lamb an innumerable multitude will stand firm for God. They can neither buy nor sell, and will probably die horrible deaths, but they come out victorious. They are rewarded with the glory of eternal service in His heavenly Temple, never to suffer hunger, thirst, tears nor heat again for ever and ever. The picture is enough to stir praise in every heart that truly loves the Lord.

Future Judgements from God: When? Where? Why? Who?

9

The New Testament tells us of three major judgements still in the future. One is in Matthew 25.31-46; one is in Romans 14.10; the third is in Revelation 20.11.

The groups of people mentioned in the three Scripture references given above are distinct and separate from each other. The time, the place, the issues, and the people are all clearly defined and distinguished, and if we fail to mark the differences we shall end in confusion, misinterpretation, and misapplication.

The idea of a *general resurrection* or a *general judgement* is not only not found in Scripture, it is anti-Scriptural, and flies in the face of the plain teachings of the Bible. John 5.28-29 clearly states that *all that are in the graves shall hear His voice*, some come forth to a resurrection of life, and others to a resurrection of judgement. There are two resurrections, for two kinds of people, with two distinct destinies involved.

Looking back to verse 24 of the same chapter we find that the believer in Christ *shall not come into judgement*. The negative is an emphatic and unconditional one, and indicates that the Christian can never be judged for his sins since these have already been judged and the sentence carried out on his Substitute at Calvary. The official receipt for this transaction, and the discharge based on it, is the resurrection of Christ

66

from the dead, Roms.4.25. So whatever these judgements may mean it cannot be that the believer will appear before a judge to answer for his sins. God has assured him that these are *put away by the sacrifice of His Son,* and that the sinner now stands completely justified and indeed accepted in that Substitute. But we must look at the judgements separately and note the distinguishing characteristics of each.

The judgement of the living nations

The judgement of Matthew 25 is said to take place when the Son of Man comes to earth and sits on His throne. The title *Son of Man* is a Millennial one, always connected with His coming to *earth* as the second man of 1 Corinthians 15.45-50 to bring all things into subjection. In the Matthew 25 passage there is no mention of a resurrection. All those involved are living nations on earth surprised in open rebellion and warfare against God. The judgement takes place on earth, and there are three groups around that throne; sheep, goats, and *these my brethren.* The company being judged is divided into sheep and goat categories according to their response to those called Christ's brethren. This leads us to identify these *brethren* as the 144,000 Jewish witnesses sealed in Revelation 7 who speak for Him after the removal of the church and during the times of sorrow and tribulation. Those who accept them and their message are blessed, and their reward is not to be taken to heaven but to *enter into the kingdom prepared for them.* Those who refuse the witnesses and their message are dismissed to everlasting fire prepared for the Devil and his angels.

The Great White Throne

Turning to Revelation 20 in the last five verses we find a completely different tribunal in surroundings and circumstances far removed from earth and living nations. Heaven and earth have passed away; the Millennial kingdom has come and gone. Satan, the Beast and the False Prophet are in the Lake of Fire as are all those who received the mark of the Beast and were judged at the coming of Christ as seen in

Matthew 25. All Christians, dead and living were taken away
from the earth at the time of the Rapture, 1 Thess.4.16,
1 Cor.15.52, and the believers who were martyred during the
Tribulation were resurrected between the Tribulation and the
Kingdom so that they could reign with Christ, Rev.20.4. The
only group remaining to be dealt with is that made up of all
who died out of Christ and unrepentant. It is these who now
stand before the Great White Throne, the final tribunal of
God.

At this judgement only those who have died and are now
raised to life appear. The company is composed of *the* dead
small and great, with no distinctions of any kind based on
human standards. These are the dead of verse 5 who, when
the martyred believers of the Tribulation were raised to reign
with Christ are said not to live again *until the thousand years*
(of the kingdom) *are finished.* There are no believers here, for
those up to the Rapture were taken away at that time and
those of the Tribulation period were raised before the kingdom, vs.4,5. So this is clearly *the resurrection of judgement*
spoken of in John 5.29.

The throne is *great* because of Him who sits on it,
because of the enormous number of people gathered before
it, and because of the issues at stake. It is *white* to remind us
of the holiness, the justice, the righteousness that charac-
terizes it. There is no escape from this final sentencing of
those who are not "in Christ", for *all* are raised and appear,
neither the depths of the oceans nor the power of the grave or
of hell itself being sufficient to withstand the command to
come forth.

Books are opened, among them the book of life, and the
Bible. This last we gather from our Lord's statement that *the
words that I speak unto you they shall judge you at the last
day,* John 12.48. What the other books may be is neither
revealed nor recorded and therefore speculation is worthless.
It is suggested that one would have to be the record of men's
works or actions, since *they are judged out of the things
written in the books, according to their works,* v.12. This is
the solemn investigation of "the record" which Job says "is

on high," Job 16.19. Nothing can be altered, or erased in that record, and there can be no suborning of this Judge. All must be faced exactly as it is.

All those whose names are not found in the book of life are cast into the Lake of Fire. This final place of punishment in total separation from God, a separation which the unbelievers have chosen for themselves during their lifetime, is described as a place of unceasing anguish which stretches on for ever and ever.

Eternal Punishment

Because of the awe-inspiring character and duration of this punishment for revolt against God, some have tried to convince themselves that it must be something less than everlasting. To bolster this reasoning they appeal to the meaning of the Greek words here used, as well as elsewhere, *aionas ton aionon* from *aion,* an age. They argue that the adjective *aionios* could mean nothing more than age long, and the phrase in Revelation 20.10 simply "to the ages of the ages" but not necessarily never-ending.

It only needs to be stated that there is no other common word in the language for everlasting; that this is constantly used in secular Greek writings and in the New Testament to convey the idea of never-ending; and that this is the word used to describe the eternal character of God Himself. If it can be proved that this word means less than everlasting when applied to the Lake of Fire, then it would have to have the same force, or same lack of it, when applied to God's existence, God's love, God's salvation, God's covenant, and even the life He gives us when we accept His salvation, to say nothing of "the eternal Spirit" Himself.

Such a passage as John 10.28, *I give unto them eternal life, and they shall never perish* loses its meaning and power, for if eternal death is not eternal, then how can we be sure that eternal life is? The two are locked together in an indissoluble equation in John 5.20, ...*His Son Jesus Christ. This is the true God and eternal life.* Here the Holy Spirit is not only stating that Jesus Christ is true God and that He *gives* or merely *has* eternal life, but that He *is* eternal life. See Genesis 21.33 where the title is El Olam, the latter word being the Hebrew synonym for the Greek aion, and compare with Psalm 90.2.

One other misconception calls for a word of explanation. Because all are alike consigned to the Lake of Fire most people have a vague notion that this represents equal or perhaps even indiscriminate punishment. The Scriptures teach otherwise. The passage we are studying says, *They were judged each separate individual according to his works,* Rev.20.12. This indicates punishment in accord with the individual's own actions. In Matthew 11.20-24 we have an added dimension, for there we are told that it is not merely a question of the isolated act in itself but also of the moral light possessed by the person committing the act. Tyre and Sidon and Sodom had all sinned. They were, and yet will be, punished for that sin, but the punishment of Chorazin, Bethsaida, and Capernaum for what we might consider less heinous offenses will be much more severe because they sinned against greater light and knowledge and therefore are much more responsible and more culpable. More privilege and enlightenment brings greater condemnation and severer punishment to those who sin in spite of them. The same truth is taught in Luke 12.47,48 where disobedience with superior knowledge demands more lashes because, says the passage, *to whomsoever much is given* (privilege) *much shall be required* (responsibility).

One more judgement remains to be studied, that of the works and service of believers with a view to reward, but this is so important a subject and has such a solemn bearing on the lives of Christians that we take a new and separate chapter to give it the attention it deserves.

10

Christian Rewards

That Christ will review the life and service of every believer in a day yet to come is a theme often touched on in the New Testament. At the time of that review He will reward faithfulness with a crown, 2 Tim.4.8; Rev.3.11 etc., and lack of devotion to Him will result in loss of reward, 1 Cor.3.15, so that this is an extremely practical subject and one often used in Scripture as a basis for exhortations to whole hearted effort for the Lord. A proper understanding of the matter will have deep and far-reaching effects in the life of any believer, so we give it a chapter to itself.

In the book of Revelation the church is not seen on earth from the end of chapter 3 until we come to chapter 19, verses 7-9. In the first Scripture we see her toiling and struggling amidst much confusion and false profession, with only a little strength, even though the Lord has put before her an open door of communion and opportunity. In all her failure the true church had still clung to His Word and His Name, and her fortitude had been rewarded and strengthened by His promise that He would keep her *out of the hour of trial which is about to come on the habitable world, to try the earth-dwellers*, Rev.3:10. To fulfil this He says He is coming quickly, v.11. This had happened, according to 1 Thessalonians 4, and 1 Corinthians 15, and now in Revelation 19 the church is seen as having made herself ready by being dressed in the royal white robes *bright and pure* (R.V.) which are said to be her own righteous acts.

These robes cannot be the righteousness with which God covers the sinner at salvation, for that is by faith, according to

71

His own sovereign grace, having nothing to do with anyone's righteous acts. It must therefore be connected with reward for her faithful service in His absence and from this and other Scriptures we gather that between Revelation 3 and 19 the church has not only been removed from earth, but gathered around the Lord Himself at the Judgement Seat and rewarded. When He comes to reign His queen consort comes with Him, and she comes to reign, having had her place of service allotted to her on the basis of her work and faithfulness, Luke 19.17. Since the place and rank of believers in the kingdom will have been appointed to them at the Judgement Seat and *before they come to earth for the Kingdom,* then this must take place between the Rapture and the Appearing. In this connection we read in Colossians 3.4, *When Christ, who is our life, shall appear, then shall ye also appear with Him* in glory.

Going back to the thought of the many exhortations in the New Testament based on this theme, Romans 14.1-13 is a notable example. Since we *shall all stand before the judgement seat of Christ, and .... every one of us shall give account of himself to God,* we are forbidden to judge or criticize our fellow Christians in their service for the Master. The passage says that only the One who died for them and commissioned them in the first place has this right to judge them. Then in 1 Corinthians 4.5 we are warned against any kind of premature judgement and told to leave this to the proper time - *when the Lord shall come.* In 1 Corinthians 3 we are reminded that the *quality* rather than the *quantity* of all work will be tested by fire in that searching evaluation, and exhorted to take great care *how* and *what* we build into our lives of service for Him. Many other practical values of this teaching could be cited but these will suffice for the moment, and others will appear as we proceed.

The ten talents

First mention of evaluation and reward for Christian service is by the Lord Himself in Luke 19.12-26 where the background is the setting up of His kingdom and, by implication, their place in it, v.11. The parable tells of a nobleman going away to receive a kingdom for himself and return. The Jewish historian Josephus tells us that Herod and his son Archelaus did this very thing, leaving Jericho where his palace was and where this parable was told, to go to Rome to be officially confirmed in the kingdom.

Before going, the nobleman distributes money among his servants, telling them to trade with it for him during his absence, implying, of course, a reckoning upon his return. In view of the sequel we are forced to believe that whatever importance the pecuniary gains may have involved, his main reason for this distribution was to sift his servants into levels of faithfulness, zeal, and application of abilities. He would need administrators in his new kingdom, and wanted to know, on the basis of performance, who fitted where, and what responsibilities each could carry. On the basis of his handling the one coin given him, each man was evaluated in a solemn and soul-searching time of accounting, and his place of responsibility in his master's new kingdom was appointed to him strictly according to his devotion, zeal, and capacity as revealed by his handling of the stewardship entrusted to him. The meaning of the story is so clear that, to an intelligent Christian, it needs no detailed application.

The writings of the Apostle Paul abound in aspirations for himself and exhortations to others in light of such a review of service and reward for it. See 1 Cor. 1.8; 4.5; 2 Cor. 1.14; Phil. 1.6, 10; 2.16; 1 Thess. 2.19; 2 Thess. 1.10; 2 Tim. 1.18; 4.8 etc., noting the term "the day of Jesus Christ," "that day," "the day," all expressions used consistently by Paul in referring to the day of accounting at the return of the Lord. There are, however, passages in which he expounds the subject in more detail and to these we must now turn.

The Lord is the Judge

In 1 Corinthians 4 the opening section deals with stewardship, or faithful dealing with that which is not our own but which has been entrusted to us by another, whom we represent, and who will require a satisfactory accounting. The Corinthians were apparently indulging in the luxury of judging

Paul in his service for God, and he informs them that their appraisal of his work is the least of his worries because they are unauthorized, unqualified, and away ahead of their time for any such thing. He adds that even he himself is not in a position to evaluate his own service. He was too close to it, too partial, and in any case all the facts and results were not in yet!

Then he reminds them that the Lord is the judge; the Coming is the time; and that with such a Judge and at such a time when the job is finished *all* will be revealed and taken into account, and then everyone will receive his proper praise from *God* and not from men. The phrasing indicates that the emphasis is not on whether *all* will receive praise or not, but that it will at that time come from *God*. The expression *He will bring to light the hidden things of darkness and will reveal the counsels of the heart* should not necessarily be restricted to the showing up of the bad. It also refers to revealing the purposes and determinations of the hearts; the struggles and wrestlings in the dark privacy of our own deep spiritual exercises; the difficulties mastered, and the sorrows borne; the failures and weaknesses dealt with and the tears hidden. Few of these things can be known or properly assessed by our fellows, or even our friends, but they are all understood by our Master, and by Him they will be given their just value.

Romans 14.1-13 deals with a similar situation though with this difference that here it is not so much a group of Christians judging a servant of God as the ugly habit of individuals criticizing each other because of different understandings of the will of God for their particular lives. The practice is condemned with the sharp words "*Who* are *you* to set yourself up as a judge?" v.4, and "*Why* are you doing it?" v.10. The words added to the last question seem to hint that the aim of the judging was merely to *despise* or *to make little of* their brother which is the meaning of the Greek word used. The aim of their judgement was to belittle; that of Christ would be to uphold and reward.

But worst of all was the fact that in judging in any

circumstances or from any motives they were usurping the place and prerogatives of the Master Himself. Christ had died for the person. Christ had commissioned him. Christ could see everything and could properly appraise all service. Christ could reward. They could do none of these and were belittling both the servant and the Master, so they are commanded to desist immediately. They are also assured that we shall *all* stand before the judgement seat of Christ, v.10, that each separate individual shall not only have opportunity for giving account of himself but shall be obliged to do so, v.12. This will be to *God* and therefore each individual should be fully assured before God as to his own motives, conduct, and understanding of the will and word of God for *himself.*

What we are

The passsage in 2 Corinthians 5.10 goes farther than saying that we shall all stand before the judgement seat. It affirms that *we must all appear* (lit. be manifested or shown up) *at the judgement seat.* In Romans 14 it is a question of being present at that tribunal; the unavoidable obligation of so doing. But in the Corinthian passage we find we are revealed, made manifest, shown up for what we really are, with no ability to hide or camouflage anything in or of ourselves. We are told elsewhere that all things are naked and open before the eyes of Him with whom we have to do, and before the Lord in that day we shall be in the open with the full light of His burning eyes upon us.

The Spirit then proceeds to say that at that complete revelation of what we are each person will receive the things done in the body *whether they be good or bad.* Some feel that the word *bad* here indicates punishment of some kind for wrongdoing or for things essentially evil. Perhaps it is worthwhile noting that there are two Greek words for bad, "kakos" and "phaulos", the first meaning bad in the sense of evil or depraved, the latter more in the sense of "worthless." Most of the texts have the latter word here in 2 Corinthians 5.10, and it must be remembered that we use the word bad for things not necessarily evil in themselves. We speak of a bad bargain, a bad investment and so on with no reference to the moral or inherent character of the thing in itself, but rather meaning that for us it was unsuitable, unprofitable, or not a very wise thing under the existing circumstances.

Perhaps in many matters where we have not actually been sinning we have nonetheless been investing ourselves and our potential, to say nothing of our time and money, in things we shall *in that day* see were bad investments. We are told plainly in Matthew 6.19 never to lay up or invest our money here on earth where it can be lost or depreciate, and where it will finally be burned up, but rather to invest it in heaven and its projects. In 1 Timothy 6.17-19 those who have money are advised to *do good* (with it) ... *be ready to distribute, willing to communicate* (share it), *laying up in store a good foundation against the time to come.* That person is wise who invests himself and all he has in God's things, for all will be investigated *at that day,* and since what we have is not ours but His we shall have to answer for it as stewards.

What we do

The next passage to be considered is 1 Corinthians 3.9-13, and here the subject is not so much what we are but what we do; our work more than our character. God has laid a foundation which is Christ and everything which the Christian as a new creature would build must be built on that foundation. That foundation *stands sure,* 2 Tim. 2.19, and can never fail. It is important, however, *how* we build on it, 1 Cor. 3.10, and *what* we build on it, v.12, since both are to be tested in a coming day by the Master architect for whose honour and glory the whole work is being done.

So we are told in verse 13 that every man (lit. each person) is given a service by the Lord and each person (same word) will have his work tested and revealed for what it is, not on the basis of quantity but rather on that of quality. Indeed the idea of quantity does not once appear in the whole passage, something which we might think about in this day when size and quantity are the usual criteria by which almost everything is checked. The standards of Christ's holiness and the high demands of that holiness will be the test of everything. Those blazing eyes, Rev.1.14, in their omniscient perceptiveness see through everything; missing nothing; deceived by nothing; misinterpreting nothing. Everything that fails to meet this high and holy standard will be burned up as unworthy of Him, and in its burning, the workman will suffer loss of reward.

The illustration used - and how the Lord delights in illustrations! - is of a great city such as Corinth was in those days, so often visited by disastrous fires. All kinds of buildings were there, from the well built and costly homes of the rich, made of valuable stones (granite and marble etc. since we do not build houses of gems) ornamented with gold and silver, right down to the hovels of the poor, the careless, or the lazy made of sticks and thatch with rubbishy straw to cover the earthen floors or stopping the chinks in the walls. As the fires swept through, every kind of building would be tested. The durable and permanent materials purchased at great cost and put in place with exhausting labour would come through unscathed. The substandard, poorly built shacks thrown together with little design and less care or work, made of shoddy materials obtained from dumps, bought for next to nothing, or maybe even pilfered from others would, when the fire passed, be little more than smouldering monuments to the folly of those who built them. Indeed, though the owners might escape with their lives they would not only lose the buildings themselves, but also everything they might have stored in them, and thus be left with nothing for the starting of the new life that lay before them.

Believers who are serving the Lord, and all believers should be, must remember that their work will be examined and tested by the Lord Himself before they are rewarded for it. At this Judgement Seat the question of the Christian's salvation or eternal security does not even come up, his destiny is never under discussion, much less his life in the hereafter. *He shall be saved,* v.15, but if his work for the Lord has been shoddy and unworthy then, like someone managing to escape from his burning home in night attire and with no chance to salvage anything else, the Christian, though safe, will bring little or nothing away for the life that lies immediately ahead. No wonder then, in view of such solemn possibilities, that *every man* is exhorted to take heed *how* he builds!

Ephesians 6.5-8 and Colossians 3.25 are addressed to Christians who were slaves receiving no pay on earth and little encouragement to do anything well, or with care and devotion. These two passages are from twin epistles written near the same time, from the same prison cell, to congregations in the same area. They tell us clearly that the most menial tasks loyally and conscientiously done for the most perverse and unappreciative of earthly masters will, if done with a heart of devotion for the Master in heaven, be amply repaid, as will failure and wrong-doing in the same context.

A study of 1 Pet.5.4; 1 Cor.9.25; Phil.4.1; 1 Thess.2.19; 2 Tim.4.8; James 1.12; Rev.2.10 is most rewarding and shows us that special and specific crowns will be awarded to servants who have been faithful in the differing labours of shepherds, runners, soul-winners, teachers, lovers of His appearing, overcomers, and martyrs. These classes of workers, embraced by the number seven of Divine completeness, probably are intended to tell us that *every* kind of service will not only be adequately rewarded, but distinctively so, though at different levels as in the parable of Luke 19, ten cities, five cities, etc.

And of course passages like 2 John 8 and others confront us with the possibility of loss of reward or failure to obtain a full reward. Other passages along the same line are 1 John 2.28; 2 Pet.1.10; Rev.3.10; Heb.13.17; 2 Tim.2.15 as well as 1 Cor.3.15 already considered.

Christ's Coming in Glory and His Kingdom on Earth

11

In order to understand what is meant by Christ's kingdom on earth, called for convenience the Millennial Kingdom because of its one thousand year duration, it is necessary to recapitulate a little to grasp the overall picture.

In Genesis 3.24 we read one of the results of the fall, or perhaps the summing up of all its results in the words, *So He* (God) *drove out the man.* In Genesis 4.1-4 we find two of Adam's sons attempting to approach God; one in God's way, *by faith,* Heb.11.4, the other in a humanistic, man-invented way. In this latter passage we have the beginning of all false religions, in a stubborn denial of the fact of sin and of God's plan for its removal. In 4.16 Cain, under the judgement of God and branded as a rebel and a murderer goes *out from the presence of God* and begins a society or civilization in revolt against God and opposed to all His plans. He builds a city, and in that new Godless society we find specifically mentioned, polygamy, v.19, agriculture and cattle raising, v.20, music, v.21, art, v.22, poetry, vs.23,24, along with murder and revenge, vs.23,24.

In this passage lie the roots of a conflict running through the ages from then until now, and destined to come to a culmination when the Deliverer promised in Genesis 3.15, the serpent-crushing seed of the woman, comes to overthrow completely the Devil's false and anti-God kingdom begun under Cain, and set up His own in its place. In Genesis 4 we have the beginning of this titanic struggle between God and

Satan, and in Revelation 19 we have its end. Let us look briefly at the overall battle picture.

In Genesis 1-2 God set up a creation and a kingdom in this world in ideal and sinless conditions. It was a true "Kingdom, or sovereignty, of the heavens," for God in heaven ruled over it all, through His delegate and viceroy Adam, in holiness, peace, and love. It was a perfect theocracy with man willing only what God willed and - *it was very good.*

The rule of Satan

But Satan aspired to steal control and lordship over this new creation, usurping the throne of world rule, and aiming at thwarting God's plans. Satan had been the head of the angelic creation, Ezekiel 28.12-15, but had fallen through the sin of pride and rebellion, Isaiah 14.12-14. To achieve his purpose, he maligned God to His creatures; convinced them that his regime of throwing off God's authority and living in self-pleasing was best for them; and won their allegiance. His was to be a rule of humanism, where man is the master as well as the centre, hub, and focus of everything, rather than God. Indeed, according to Satan they *would be as God,* which means that his target and goal was the deification of man. We should keep this clearly in mind as we proceed.

Nebuchadnezzar's crowning sin and folly was in a denial, at first, *that the Most High ruleth in the kingdoms of men.* Psalm 2 shows man's basic sin as one of rebellion in saying, *Let us break their bands asunder, and cast away their cords from us* referring to the restraints and harness of God.

And in the end times it is Satan's throne that is given to the Beast, as we have already seen, so that Satan is really making a last bid to take the place of God, ruling the world through *his* viceroy, who in reality is his dupe and tool and who at that time will set up his image in the Temple in Jerusalem claiming *that he is God.* At this point humanism will have reached the peak of its ambitious plans, when God has lost the allegiance of the bulk of His creatures and is, in fact, ruled out of His own creation and displaced from His own Temple in worship.

When, in the Gospels, the Son came to summon it all back to God as His kingdom, He was murdered. When He comes back again to restore it by force to God, that triumvirate of evil, Satan, the Beast and the False Prophet, become the channels of a demon invasion which deludes the kings of the earth to join in a final battle to deny Him entry or authority. See Revelation 16.13-16 with 19.19.

As far back as the times of Abraham Satan had so corrupted man that the nations, as such, were "given up" by God, Roms.1.24,26,28. He chose Abraham to begin a new nation for Himself; His own treasure, a people peculiarly His own. But again Satan set about defeating this plan and led Israel away after demon-idols so that God was obliged to deliver His people to the captivities of Assyria and Babylon, and the *times of the Gentiles* began.

The rule of Christ

Of course God had not given up His eternal purposes. He made the king of Babylon learn and confess that even in these circumstances *the Most High God ruleth in the kingdom of men and giveth it to whomever He will, setting over it the basest of men,* Dan.4.17. Even the knowledge of the course of such world rule is known only to God and to those to whom He chooses to reveal it, Dan.2.18,28,29. And the end of all such revelation is that God's rule must finally be re-established on earth. We have already glanced at this in our study of Daniel chapters 2, 7, 9, and 11.

As we have seen above in passing, when the fulness of the time had come God sent His Son, the Anointed or Messiah, to His own kingdom or house, but His own people received Him not, John 1.11. Instead of a crown and a throne He was given the thorns and the cross where He died to be a propitiation for the sins of the whole world, 1 John 2.2, and to lay the foundation for the cleansing of the whole kingdom against the day when He would come back again to take it by force.

While Christ was on earth the Devil made Him an offer of the kingdoms of the earth on his own terms, underlining his own plans in a paraphrase, or perhaps a parody, of Jehovah's words which we have already cited from Daniel 4.17, by saying, *It is delivered to me and I give it to whomever I will,* Luke 4.6. So the battle lines are drawn for the fight as to who shall have the kingdom and how it shall be governed. Christ refused the kingdom as offered by Satan, but the arch-enemy of God will offer it to the Beast who will accept it. And just as God's own King who came in His Father's name was refused, so the imposter coming in his own name at the last days will be received by a blinded world, John 5.43.

When the Lord comes back again to earth in glory and power, Zech. 14.1,2; Matt. 24.30; Rev. 19.11-21, it is to smash this rebellious world system and its rulers under Satan, Dan. 2.44; 7.26, sweep it completely away, Dan. 2.35, and set up something entirely new and divine. This will not be a kingdom which absorbs that which it overcomes and replaces, as is usually the case historically in worldly conquest. It is altogether from above in character. Furthermore it does not come in gradually or through preaching or conversion, much less by an improvement of conditions on earth. It is brought in by devastating blows of justice from God, in which wilful Israel, the godless Gentile nations, the Harlot church, the Beast, the False Prophet and Satan who is the mastermind behind it all, are dealt with by a holy God.

The progressive improvement theme has long been taught and believed in mainline establishment theology. It is, in fact, part of the product of humanistic thinking in modernist "liberal" Christendom, and is without a single word of Bible authority. Even one of our musically beautiful hymns speaks of the kingdom coming through "a story we have to tell to the nations which shall turn their hearts to the right" because "the darkness shall turn to dawning and the dawning to noonday bright, and God's great kingdom shall come on earth; the kingdom of love and light." That hymn, we regret to say, is both in its concept and its expression a total fallacy and misinterpretation of Scripture, and if we do not believe it there is no reason why we should sing it.

After the battle of Armageddon as described in Revelation 19 the Beast and the False Prophet are thrown alive into the Lake of Fire. Their followers are judged and dismissed into everlasting punishment, Matt.25.46, and the Devil is chained in the abyss, Rev.20.1,2. This is done because there could be no Millennium with these on the loose. Then the Lord's people enter the kingdom with Him where they reign with Him for one thousand years. Read 1 Cor.6.2; 2 Tim.2.12; Matt.25.34; Rev.20.4. We must now consider the Millennial Kingdom itself and conditions during its course.

The Millennial Kingdom

The word "Millennium" does not occur in the Bible but five times in Revelation 20 Christ's kingdom is referred to as running *on earth* for one thousand years. Since "mil" is a recognized Latinism for one thousand the word was coined or rather Anglicized as a short and convenient name for the reign of "mil annum" or one thousand years.

Topographical changes

Many startling changes are predicted for the earth during the period of Christ's reign. It is promised that *the desert shall bloom like a rose* and some seem to think that this is already finding some kind of fulfilment in a more fertile and productive Palestine in the hands of the sophisticated, inventive, and energetic Israelis. But the millennial fertility will not result from the labours of unbelieving Jews, but rather from God and the direct rule of His Son.

Zechariah 14 clearly teaches that there will be far-reaching changes in the topographical and geological structure of the land of Palestine when the Lord comes. As His feet touch the Mount of Olives that whole mountain formation shall be torn apart, leaving an enormous chasm or canyon running east and west from the Mediterranean Sea to the Jordan valley. This valley, the northern part of the famous Great Rift Valley, will be elevated so that the Dead Sea, now almost 1,300 feet below sea level, will at last drain. Its waters will be "healed" so that all fish found in the Mediterranean and elsewhere will flourish in it, Ezek. 47.1-12, with a great river flowing from Jerusalem west to the Mediterranean and east through the Dead Sea to the Gulf of Aquaba and the Red Sea, Zech. 14.8. As the valleys rise the mountains will sink, so that the whole land surface will become one great and fertile plain, Zech. 14.10.

Agricultural changes

Isaiah 35.1,2; Joel 3.18; and Amos 9.13 as well as others, predict a period of agricultural productivity never known before. In it *the plowman shall overtake the reaper, and the treader of grapes him that soweth seed, and the mountains shall drop sweet wine, and all the hills shall melt*, i.e., dissolve, in the abundance of wine, oil and honey. Joel says, *The hills shall flow with milk, and all the rivers of Judah shall flow with waters, and a fountain shall come forth from the house of the Lord and shall water the valley of Shittim.* These quotations and many others show that the curse on the ground of Genesis 3 will be removed, and man will learn the wisdom of God regarding the use of God's earth. There will be a time of accelerated productivity in new climatic and topographic conditions when, with altered seasons, all year round will be time for sowing and harvesting.

Changed living conditions

In such conditions of plenty, personal living will be of a totally different quality also. Isaiah 65 gives us an outline of wonderful conditions in the Millennium and in verse 18 we are told that along with this great abundance of everything from the land, but not dependent on it, will come gladness and true joy, with weeping and crying banished.

Verse 20 means that there will neither be premature death nor early decay, though the rebellious sinner will be accursed, or cut off, in the governmental dealings of a righteous Judge. Cf. Psalm 101.8.

We are assured in verses 21 and 22 of Isaiah 65 that

those who build will live therein, and those who cultivate will eat and enjoy the produce with no fear of loss, frustration, or foreclosure. In our society people often produce for others what they cannot afford for themselves; or, having produced or acquired are forced to surrender to others through adverse circumstances, sometimes unjust, over which they have no control. All this will vanish under the righteous yet benign rule of the Lord Jesus. Psalm 72 shows that under that rule will be perfect justice and equitable distribution for all, without reference to social or economic position. Graft, corruption, privilege, and favouritism will be impossible under such authority.

Verse 23 tells us that all labour will be adequately rewarded, verse 24 that perfect spiritual communication with God through prayer will be the order of the day, with wayward, selfish desires removed, and prayer always in the will of God and therefore always answered positively.

From Micah 4.4 we learn that every man shall sit under his own vine and his own fig tree and this without fear of molestation from anyone. This is surely a comforting thought in an age when such fear is almost universal, and when, even if one sits under a tree of any sort it is likely to be state owned, or at least controlled, rather than one's own, or maybe made of plastic. The same passages state clearly that during the Millennium, Israel and Jerusalem will be the centre of all moral teaching, Micah 4.2, as well as of world government. This teaching and government, as well as the Lord's presence and power will lead to a -

Complete eradication of war

This condition will be for the whole world, v.3, and will include the conversion of all war potential and production to profitable and peaceful ends.

Changes in the animal creation

Just as the curse which was pronounced on the ground because of sin in Genesis 3 shall be removed under the rule of Christ, so too the enmity between man and beast shall cease.

In the beginning God gave Adam dominion over the whole of the brute creation. The animals were all brought to him to be named, apparently in submission to him for we read in Psalm 8 that he has *under his feet* not only domestic animals but also the beasts of the field, and the fish and fowl as well. And yet, in Hebrews 2.8, referring to and quoting from this very Psalm it is said, *but now we see not yet all things subjected to him.* Because of sin man has lost his control, and is in conflict with the animal creation which, "all red in tooth and claw," is often his mortal enemy. Romans 8.19-23 shows not only man *made subject to vanity* and waiting for deliverance, but *the whole creation groaning.*

But just as everything has turned to vanity and violence through the sin of the first man, so under the dominion of *the second man,* that is Christ, all will again be brought into subjection and peace. And so the prophet sang, *The wolf shall dwell with the lamb, the leopard shall lie down with the kid, the calf, and the lion and the fatling together, and a little child shall lead them. The cow and the bear shall feed, their young ones shall lie down together, the lion shall eat straw like an ox. And the sucking child shall play on the hole of the asp, and the weaned child shall put his hand in the adder's den. They shall not hurt nor destroy in all my holy mountain for the earth shall be full of the knowledge of the Lord as the waters cover the sea,* Isa. 11.6-9.

The Eternal State:
the sevenfold consummation
of the purpose of God

To round out our rapid survey of Bible prophecy we must glance briefly at Revelation 22.3-5 where, it seems to this writer, we have spelled out in short but pregnant phrases the character and conditions of the eternal state, which we usually refer to as *heaven*.

The one thousand year kingdom of Christ on earth has run its course; Satan has been released for a short time from the abyss and has deceived the unregenerate people born during that period into a revolt against the Lord, only to be swept away in fiery retribution. Satan is now in the Lake of Fire, his permanent place of punishment, where the Beast and the False Prophet have been since the end of the Tribulation, that is for more than one thousand years. At the end of chapter 20 the last judgement, that of the unrepentant dead, takes place, thus winding up the whole story. Then in 21.1-8 we have the new heaven and the new earth and so enter on the Eternal State. The remainder of that chapter appears to be a flashback to an earlier epoch giving a description of *the Bride*, the Lamb's wife coming down out of heaven to show us her relationship with earth. We have already seen several instances, particularly in chapter 12, of this same kind of thing projecting us sometimes backward and sometimes forward, for a view of the origins, relationships, and character of leading personalities in the drama. The story then, in chapter 22, reverts to the Eternal State.

Let us consider the seven points of that concise description, or rather characterization, in the order given:

1) There shall be no more curse - perfect sinlessness.
2) The throne of God - perfect rule and authority.

3) His servants shall serve Him - perfect obedience.
4) They shall see His face - perfect communion.
5) His name on them - perfect consecration.
6) No night there - perfect blessedness.
7) They shall reign for ever and ever - perfect glory.

Down through the years many theological debates have raged about Heaven, its location, its inhabitants, its conditions of life, its joys etc. There have also been some bitter disputes about some of these things, and also about the literalness or otherwise of some of the descriptions given: harps, robes, crowns, seas of glass, thrones, altars, rainbows and so on. The Scriptures themselves give few answers to these questions, and where Scripture is silent we do well to avoid imaginative speculation which, as well as being useless, can actually be misleading and even dangerous.

Indescribable

Many of our hymns have, with the best of intentions in the saintliest of writers, only added to the confusion by applying to the eternal state descriptions which rightly belong to the Millennium, the church in the Millennium, the kingdom of heaven etc. So we have "the city four square in the land of fadeless day," "the golden streets of heaven on which all men hope to walk one day," "Immanuel's land" etc.

In 2 Corinthians 12.2-4 Paul refers to being caught up to the third heaven or paradise, but makes no attempt to describe what he *saw*, while what he *heard* was *not lawful to be uttered* because it was *unspeakable*. Passages like this should warn us that God has drawn a line as to what can be communicated to us within the bounds of our comprehension about that place of unutterable joy and blessing, for the present at least. Earth's vocabulary has been developed to handle earthly phenomena, but there exist on earth no words for that world which is so "other" to everything we know or have words to describe.

It may also be that God has been trying to guard against our tendency to become unduly preoccupied with some kind of Christian Nirvana or Never-never-land which would lessen our appreciation of what we *now* have in Christ, and our responsibility to live in it and for it. We so quickly jump at escape from reality. And of course most of these discussions have centred around the *physical and material* aspects of heaven, often to the exclusion, or at least the ignoring of the fact that God is Spirit and therefore His eternal abode would be a place where the emphasis would be on the spiritual concept and condition.

One other not very healthy aspect of these imaginings is that they are almost entirely taken up with the selfish angle of heaven; what *we* shall see, and feel, and have, and enjoy. What it will be like to *us*? Will *we* know this, or that, or the other? Little of God's side seems to enter into our thinking.

In Revelation 22.3-5 we have the most detailed statement given anywhere of that glorious time and place and it is not surprising that it is given almost entirely in terms of spiritual and moral character and condition, at the same time giving proper prominence to the Godward aspect. Let us then consider the seven statements one by one and try to learn something from them.

1] There shall be no more curse.

There are many curses in the Bible, some individual, some racial, some spiritual, some physical, but all full of deadly meaning. All spring from sin, and flow from those first curses in Genesis 3 pronounced on Satan, the serpent, the ground etc. as a result of the intrusion of sin into God's creation. Abraham was told in Genesis 12.3 that a curse would rest on all who would oppose God's plans for Israel, and in Galatians 1.8,9 the Holy Spirit through Paul lays a curse on anyone perverting the Gospel or preaching a different one. Finally, in the end of Revelation 22 a curse is pronounced on him who would add to or take from the now completed Bible. In between these the range and variety of curses is great, and forms material for much study outside our scope at this time. It is, however, abundantly clear that they all stem from that rebellion against God in the Garden of Eden with its resultant wrong-doing and evil, and they all lie like a blanket of judgement on mankind.

What a joy to know that in the presence of God for the ages of eternity sin and its consequences will be forever removed! And what cause for worship and adoration to realize that its removal is the work of our Lord Jesus Christ alone! Thorns and thistles were the very emblems and proofs of the curse in Genesis 3. Again, *Cursed is everyone that hangeth on a tree,* Deut. 21.22,23 with Gal. 3.13. And so we see our Divine Substitute crowned with thorns and hanging on a tree. He was made a curse for us that for ever and ever there should be in that wonderful place *no more curse.*

2] *The Throne of God and of the Lamb shall be in it.*

In Eden the basis of all happiness, enjoyment and peace, indeed the basis of everything, was the recognition of God's sovereign authority, and the necessity for complete obedience to God's word. This was the keystone that held everything together, and for this reason Satan must undermine that authority and produce disobedience to that word.

God's word was questioned - Hath God said?

His authority was denied - Ye shall not surely die.

His motives were impugned - God knows ... ye shall
be as gods.

Man accepted Satan's word against God's, and by implication he accepted Satan's authority as well. In this way Satan usurped a place and was given a power in this world that were not rightly his. He became the god of this world; the prince of the power of the air, the prince of this world, the spirit that now operates in those characterized by disobedience, Eph. 2.2. He was also able to say to the Incarnate Creator, referring to the kingdoms of this world and their glory, *It has been given over to me; and I give it to whomever I wish,* Luke 4.6.

From the moment of Satan's usurpation of authority and man's acceptance of it in doing what he thought was his own will, onwards through the whole course of world history, chaos has been the result. His introductory promise, *Ye shall be as gods* formed the foundation of humanism under whatever guise it has paraded from century to century. The enthronement of man has been his own basic philosophy ever since, albeit camouflaged and in a variety of systems and packages. It underlies the actions of great empire builders from the Pharaohs to the petty leaders of some of the emerging countries who have prohibited the preaching of original sin because it degrades man, undermines his confidence in himself, and detracts from his personal dignity. Humanism underlies the Communist dialectic - God dethroned and debunked; man in His place ruling the world. Socialism, state or otherwise, republicanism, even the concept of democracy - the rule of the people - all have their roots in the same principle, that Man can run God's universe without God Himself. Renaissance Man, as he was and is proudly called, started the last historical impulse in this direction with his cry of intellectual and spiritual emancipation, the unchaining of the human spirit, etc. That was the time of the great blossoming of art and inspiration after the wilderness of the Dark Ages, when learning surged forward and man saw himself at last *free*. It was also the time of the most monstrous licentiousness, graft, corruption, intrigue, and evil that had been seen in ages.

Humanism

This Humanism is the very basic material of true republicanism with its proud boast of "complete confidence in the rightness and soundness of the common man" and his inherent right to shape his own destiny.

Probably the high-water mark up to the present in humanistic organization in world government is the United Nations Organization, and it is significant that in that body, which undertakes to bring in *peaceful world government* and which, through its many satelite bodies (World Health, Unesco, World Court, World Bank and World Monetary Fund) meddles in life at every level, officially bars prayer or any recognition of God or His Son from all its public gatherings.

It is to this rejection of the rule and authority of God that we may trace and attribute all of earth's sorrows and woes; its violence and crime; the ruination of its educational systems; the wars, injustices, famines, and disruptions. Here we find the key to its lawlessness, corruption, and degeneration within its own structure and in all its functions, until as the Word says, *The whole creation groans and writhes in birth pangs,* Roms. 8.22.

And it will be for this very reason that Heaven will be Heaven, for there the rightful sovereignty of God will be re-established and the very hub of that place of peace will be a righteous and stable throne from which a God who is love will rule over a new creation with those who love Him in return and know that His rule is for their very best interests. And again the glory will all go to Christ and His death and resurrection, as we read in Romans 14.9, *For to this end Christ both died and lived again, that He might be Lord both of the dead and living.*

3] *His servants shall serve Him.*

The concept of God's home as some kind of heavenly Hawaii where His people lounge eternally on celestial beaches, or an everlasting old people's home or retirement centre, is contrary to Scripture and repugnant to spiritual minds. Adam in Eden was not an unoccupied, aimless enjoyer (otherwise known as a parasite along for what it can get, without responsibility or effort). He was a gloriously busy, constantly employed viceroy, running the creation for God. We find him naming animals, ruling, subduing, tending, and all as God's representative and in communion with Him.

Man's greatest mistake, and earth's greatest calamity was his refusal to serve God, and his voluntary subjection of himself to Satan, *fulfilling the desires of the flesh and the mind,* Eph.2.3.

By the same token when men accept Christ's salvation and lordship their first aspiration is to take His yoke upon them in dedicated service. This service is, alas, often marred by slowness of understanding, lack of zeal, weakness of body, and the very limitations to which we, as humans, are subject. But in the eternal state we shall serve Him uninterruptedly and fully, without ever failing to understand His wishes, without frailty of body or weariness of mind, and in all possibility we shall not be restricted by factors of time, space and motion as down here, but, like the angels, shall move freely throughout His whole renewed universe on wings of joy impelled by unsinning and undiminishing zeal for the ages of the ages.

4] *They shall see His face.*

One of the results of original sin was the expulsion of man from the presence of God, and from the ecstasy of constant and direct communion with Him. Because of sin man hid in shame. Then God drove him out as morally incapable of communicating with Him in his sinful condition. This is spiritual death: isolation from God. The prodigal son, wilfully cut off from contact with his father, was said to be *dead*. Adam, by sin, died as God said he would. He could, and still does, communicate with the physical around him through his body, but since he had died spiritually he could not communicate with God - he was dead because of sin.

God said much later, through Isaiah in 59.2, that Israel's sins and iniquities had separated between them and God and had hidden His face from them that He would not hear. The sinner is said in Ephesians 4.18 to be *alienated from the life of God through ignorance* and in Colossians 1.21, *Alienated in your mind by wicked works.* Having rejected God's offer of reconciliation through the Gospel and so fixed his position as an enemy, man reaches the final point where that rejection is punished by dismissal from God's presence in the words, *Depart from me,* and such *shall go away into outer darkness.* This is the very essence of Hell - eternal separation and isolation from God, who is the source of all life, peace, joy, and satisfaction.

And so this middle and pivotal characteristic of heaven is the restoration of communion with God. It is seeing God again with no cloud between. It is being purified so that we can enjoy His holiness, the holiness of light unapproachable. It is communing with Him, sharing His thoughts, His affections, His plans. Peter speaks of Christ as One whom *having not seen, we love,* and the very high-water mark of joy in eternity will be to find ourselves "face to face with Christ our Saviour."

5] *His name shall be in their foreheads.*

We write our name on something which is exclusively ours, and it is in this way shown plainly to be ours, and identified by all as for our use and enjoyment. In describing

His own desires and purposes in the choosing of Israel, God said it was that the nation should be His *peculiar treasure.* In the same way He said some five times in the prophetic books that He had "called Israel by His name."

God's name engraved or sealed on anyone or anything also speaks of inviolable security. His name upon them was His pledge to Israel that underneath would always be His everlasting arms, and over them His spread wings.

But above and beyond all these ideas, God's name stands for His character, Himself, what He *is* essentially. Therefore to have His name on us is to be associated with Him in His character, indeed, to have His very character engraved on us.

This was God's original intention, but how different things turned out because of sin! Man revolted against God and withdrew from His allegiance, denying God's right of possession. Cain went out from the presence of God, not marked as God's own possession, but branded for punishment. The image of God's holiness was, before long, blotted out in men who walk *according to the prince of the power of the air.* So far as being secure in God's care is concerned, it is the last thing man wants in his natural condition.

But once salvation is appropriated by the sinner he is brought back to God in reconciliation, surrendering to Him in a glad and total identification with Christ *who did always those things which pleased God.* He at once knows himself to be personally God's treasure, Titus 2.14; 1 Pet.2.9; indeed, he wants to be conformed to the image of God's Son. He wants to belong to God; to be set apart for God's use, to present himself to God, Roms.12.1, to feel and know the security which comes from being possessed by Him and protected by Him eternally.

All of this, however much it may be yearned for, is only partially enjoyed in this life, and is always marred by sin and imperfection as the old nature battles to assert itself. But up there, having been made like Him through seeing Him as He is, we shall have His character stamped upon us, His full possession of us realized, and our eternal security fully manifested to heaven, earth, and hell as, in His presence, we are marked as exclusively His, and ever and only for His use.

6] *No night there.*

God is light, and His creature, man, can never find true light apart from Him. Darkness and night in Scripture always speak of doubt, ignorance, separation, and the state and quality of being lost - shut off from the true light. In Romans 1.21 man, by turning away from the knowledge of God, found his senseless heart darkened (RV). The Word of God portrays him as *in darkness*, Romans 2.19, walking in it, 1 John 1.6, loving it, John 3.19, producing works characterized by it, Romans 13.12, under its authority, Colossians 1.13 (RV), and in Ephesians 5.8 he is actually said to *be* darkness just as God in another place is said to *be* light. Stubborn refusal of the light will in the end land him in *outer darkness*, Matt.22.13.

For the believer, however, even now all is changed. God who commanded the light to shine out of darkness in Genesis 1, has shone into his heart, and there is now a new light there, the light of the glory of God shining in the face of Jesus Christ, 2 Cor.4.6. He has been called out of the darkness, 1 Pet.2.9, is no longer *of* it, 1 Thess. 5.5, and does not walk in it any longer, John 8.12. True, he lives in a place of darkness as long as he is in this world, but he has the Word of God as a light, Psalm 119.105; 2 Pet.1.19, and his eyes are fixed on the horizon where the Day Star must shortly arise. And then at last, with sin completely taken away as a result of the work of Christ in the terrible darkness of Calvary, comes the time when there is no need of any created luminary. The distance is bridged, the darkness is removed, man is purified and can rejoice in endless light, and in that endless day where God's glory and beauty and holiness shine out unhindered and unclouded there shall never again be darkness for He Himself is the light of that holy place. This will be pure bliss.

7] *They shall reign for ever.*

In the garden, as God's viceroy and representative Adam was to have dominion over the whole creation. He was to lead it all forward in blessing under the benign rule of its Creator in perfection, peace, and joy.

Instead of raising himself by his sin, he became a slave, and the creation he was to have led in blessing he caused to be cursed and polluted. It also became such that he could only wrest sustenance from it by sweat and toil. From that moment man's rule has been a ruined one, with the greatest of leaders ending in frustration and failure, while the most promising systems of government peter out in decline and darkness. All earth's fondest hopes disintegrate in flaming chaos under its last human ruler, the Beast, and then God sweeps it all away to make room for *the second man,* Christ, and a whole new order of men. He, by His own work and worth cleanses, heals, restores, and subdues. While He rules over a renewed earth for one thousand years His people rule with Him, and then this earthly kingdom merges into its final and eternal form in the New Heaven and New Earth. Then all will be under the rule of the perfect, and therefore last, Adam, that is Christ. All those whom He has redeemed and who have therefore been transformed into His likeness, shall share in that glorious reign, as we have already shown. To reign with Christ eternally is the sum of all glory.

Since sin can never again intrude, there can be no interruption this time, and the glory of it will go on and on as they reign with Him for the ages that know no end.

In this seven-fold consummation of God's plan for His creation we have seen that all of it, with its benefits and blessings and its glory for God, flows entirely from Christ and His work on the cross, and this is why the song of that wonderful place will forever be:

> *Thou art worthy*
> *for Thou wast slain,*
> *and hast redeemed us to God*
> *by Thy blood.*

Rev. 5.9